THE BOOK OF
WEEDS

THE BOOK OF
WEEDS

Ken Thompson

LONDON, NEW YORK, MUNICH,
MELBOURNE, DELHI

Project Editor Annelise Evans
Project Art Editor Clare Shedden
U.S. Editor Beth Landis Hester

Senior Editor Helen Fewster
Pearson Picture Library Lucy Claxton
Picture Research Jo Walton
Jacket Design Mark Cavanagh
Production Luca Frassinetti
Senior Managing Editor Anna Kruger
Managing Art Editor Alison Donovan
Indexer Michèle Clarke

Photographers Peter Anderson, Andy Crawford
Illustrator Francesca Gormley

First American Edition, 2009

Published in the United States by
DK Publishing
375 Hudson Street
New York, New York 10014

09 10 11 12 10 09 08 07 06 05 04 03 02 01

[TD415—April 09]

Published in Great Britain by Dorling Kindersley Limited

A catalog record for this book is available from the Library of Congress.

ISBN 978-0-7566-4271-6

DK books are available at special discounts when purchased in bulk
for sales promotions, premiums, fund-raising, or educational use.
For details, contact: DK Publishing Special Markets, 375 Hudson Street,
New York, New York 10014 or SpecialSales@dk.com.

Printed and bound by Hung Hing, China

Discover more at
www.dk.com

Foreword

They say that by the time we're 40, we all have the faces we deserve: if you smile a lot, your face naturally relaxes into cheery creases, but if you're often miserable, you'll look it. Much the same applies to your weeds. The fussy, tidy gardener, forever hoeing, mowing, and pruning, is troubled only by the nimble annual weeds that need the bare earth created by all that activity.

The laissez-faire gardener, in contrast, is prey to all the big, spreading perennial weeds that thrive on neglect. But although he or she has the worse weeds, they worry about them less. Nor do they lose sleep over pearlwort or thale cress, weeds of such diffidence that the gardeners are quite unaware of their existence.

Whether you occupy either of these extremes or, like most of us, you're somewhere in the middle, this book is for you. The first part should help you to understand why weeds are so infuriatingly successful, while the second offers some general thoughts on weed control. Only then do I try to offer specific advice on particular weeds.

By the end of the book you may have come, if not to love them, at least grudgingly to admire weeds. You may even have decided that there are some weeds you can live with, and so be better able to direct your fire at those you can't. Either way, good luck and good weeding.

Ken Thompson

Contents

What is it about weeds?
Unwanted, unappealing, unrelenting

What is a weed?

The *Shorter Oxford English Dictionary* says that a weed is "a plant that grows, especially profusely, where it is not wanted," which captures some of the spirit of weediness, but I think not all of it. One idea this definition conveys is that any plant can be a weed, if it's in the wrong place.

If you garden on acidic soil, the pretty, pink-flowered shrub sheep laurel (*Kalmia angustifolia*) may be one of your most prized possessions. If you're a Canadian blueberry farmer, kalmia could be one of your worst nightmares and you may spend thousands of dollars every year burning or poisoning it. If *any* plant in the wrong place can be a weed, it's not a very promising start to a book on weeds, is it?

Some plants are much more likely than others to fall into the "not wanted" category. There are plenty of places where *Kalmia* is wanted: I know, because I paid good money for the one in my garden. On the other hand, it's hard to think of anywhere that, say, docks or field horsetail would actually be wanted. Tolerated maybe, but wanted? No. There's a value judgement here, which has a lot to do with aesthetics—kalmia is attractive, docks and horsetail certainly aren't—but this isn't quite as simple as it looks.

Beauty is not only in the eye of the beholder, it also has a lot to do with fashion; a plant can go from prizewinner to pariah (and back again) in less time than it takes to visit the garden center.

Is it enough to be ugly and in the wrong place? I don't think so.

A clue lies in the *SOED* phrase "especially profusely." Proper weeds—the ones worth worrying about—are also difficult to control. John Burroughs, the American naturalist, wrote in 1896 that

> Perhaps the most notable thing about the weeds that have come to us from the old world...is their persistence, not to say pugnacity.... Our native weeds are for the most part shy and harmless....

While his complaint about the bad behavior of many European plants when transplanted to the New World is quite justified, he wasn't being entirely honest about the native American flora. Many are far from shy and harmless. Indeed, a "shy and harmless weed" is an oxymoron.

Real weeds—the ones this book is about—are the opposite of shy, and I suspect it's this very belligerence that upsets many gardeners, even more than any actual harm caused. Especially for those of a tidy disposition, the insult caused by weeds—the implication that you're not in control—is worse than the injury.

Takeover tactics

Implicit in weediness is the idea of rapid expansion, of unpredictability, of an ability to turn up anywhere and quickly turn a bridgehead into an army of occupation. How do bad weeds (or good ones, depending on your point of view) do this? Essentially in one of two ways: by seeds or by vegetative reproduction from spreading stems or roots—although some can do both.

HIGH-SPEED WEEDS

Many bad weeds produce lots of seeds, and the worst ones do this very quickly. We don't know the identity of the fastest-growing plant because they haven't all been measured, but annual meadow grass can go from germination to ripe seeds in less than a month. Some annual weeds are even faster, which is why they are often called "ephemerals."

Partly this is our fault, since it is the fastest-seeding individuals that escape our attempts at control and then pass on their abilities to their offspring.

In its natural habitat, thale cress can be a well-behaved "winter annual" of rock outcrops; its strategy is to occupy very shallow soils that dry out completely in summer. It does this by germinating in fall, growing very slowly during the winter and then flowering, seeding, and dying in spring. This rather inflexible life cycle depends on fixed responses of both seeds and plants to temperature and day length in its natural habitats. Once thale cress escaped into gardens, it quickly evolved the ability to germinate and flower almost all year round and to compress its life cycle into a very short time indeed.

Not surprisingly, thale cress has become the plant of choice for plant geneticists who wanted a botanical version of the fruit fly—a plant that would happily get through eight or ten generations in a year. Having seen it in action in my garden, I think they made the right choice. Related to thale cress, but

even more
infuriating,

is hairy bittercress, with ripe seed pods that explode as soon as you touch them, shooting seeds in all directions.

Whether they spread by seeds or vegetative methods, above ground or below, or are annual or perennial—in good conditions,

rapid growth
is almost a *sine qua non*
of a **bad weed**.

Successful weeds have to keep one step ahead of the gardener's attempts at control. Admittedly, those attempts may vary from the assiduous to the downright lackadaisical, but no really slow-growing weed can hope to get the better of any but the most apathetic gardener.

In this respect, garden weeds differ fundamentally from weeds in the countryside, where slow-growing weeds, free from any frequent attempt at control, can—and do—cause considerable problems. Sheep laurel and the purple-flowered *Rhododendron ponticum* are just too slow-growing to cause much trouble in the average garden.

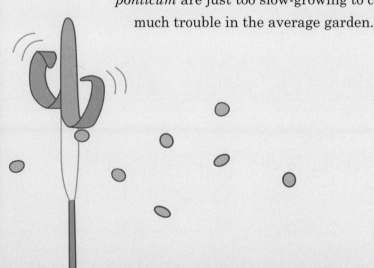

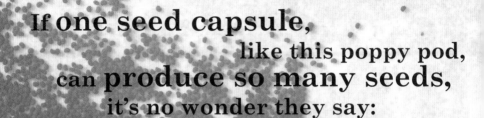

If one seed capsule,
like this poppy pod,
can **produce so many seeds,**
it's no wonder they say:

**one year's seed,
seven years' weeds**

SEEDS OF PERSISTENCE

The worst annual weeds may be very short-lived, but sadly their seeds are not. The seeds of hairy bittercress, thale cress, and of many plants like them are tiny (thale cress seeds weigh only 0.02 milligrams each), numerous, and very long-lived in soil. This longevity has two consequences. The obvious one is that they are almost impossible to eradicate; the less obvious result is that they eventually end up everywhere—moved around on boots, tools, and machinery, and in soil and compost.

Collect soil from almost anywhere that has ever been cultivated and it's a good bet that you'll find in it the seeds of pearlwort. Probably by means of seeds in or on packing cases, pearlwort has managed to colonize even Gough Island in the South Atlantic and Marion Island in the Indian Ocean, two of the most remote and isolated specks of land on the planet.

GOING TO SEED

Dispersing seeds on the wind to colonize new areas
is a speciality of the daisy family: dandelions,
groundsel, ragwort, and sowthistles are familiar
examples of weeds that do this, but there are many
others. Unrelated to daisies, but equally effectively
dispersed, are several species of willowherb.

The parachutes of dandelion or willowherb seeds are so
efficient that their tiny seeds are lifted up into the air by the
slightest turbulence or convection, and they can then travel
long distances. Even so, most seeds don't get very far:

- 99.5 percent of dandelion seeds travel less than
  11 yards (10 meters)
- only 0.05 percent go farther than 110 yards (100 meters)
- a mere 0.014 percent exceed 1,094 yards (1 kilometer).

That sounds like good news until you realize that a healthy
dandelion population may contain more than 700,000 plants in
a mere two and a half acres (one hectare). If each plant produces
200 seeds per flowerhead, that's 140,000,000 seeds, which means
about 20,000 seeds even ⅗ mile (1 kilometer) away.

So if you've ever wondered why your garden is never free
of dandelions, despite your best efforts, now you know.

Willowherb seedhead with seed "parachutes."

HITCHING A RIDE

Traveling miles on the wind or living for decades in the soil does not exhaust the tricks available to weed seeds. The brittle, scrambling goosegrass has seeds covered with tiny hooks, as is the entire plant. If goosegrass isn't in your garden already, it's all too easy to bring its large seeds back on your socks or sweater after a walk. For an annual weed, goosegrass is slow to flower, which ought to give you time to deal with it, but its climbing ability allows it to grow to maturity unseen inside a hedge or shrub.

Other weeds that get around on socks include wood avens (*Geum urbanum*), which is even harder to remove, and many weed grasses; the hairy seeds of Yorkshire fog (*Holcus lanatus*) are particularly good at this. Surprisingly, so are dandelion and its relatives—the parachute may have evolved as an aid to wind dispersal, but it's quite good at sticking to all things wooly too. Hitchhiking on socks is not the only way

weed seeds can invade your garden.

Left to right: **Goosegrass burrs** cling fast to socks, **weed seedlings** of holly, ivy, and yew.

Many plants solicit the assistance of birds by wrapping their seeds in sweet, fleshy fruits. Sometimes the bird carries the fruit away and just drops the seeds or, more often, it eats the whole lot and excretes the seeds later. Either way, the seed gets a ride to a new site. The beauty of this arrangement, from the plant's perspective, is that birds can carry seeds that are too big to be moved easily by wind.

Bird-dispersed seeds usually belong to shrubs and trees, which are too slow-growing to be really troublesome weeds, but even so they can't be ignored. My garden would long ago have been completely taken over by holly and ivy if I didn't keep pulling up the seedlings.

ROOT OF THE PROBLEM

Seeds provide one of the best ways for plants
to travel long distances; for annuals (which die
after flowering), they are the only way of getting
anywhere. But perennials have evolved a whole
armory of aids to local expansion, some of them
becoming feared weeds in the process.

Rooting stems Many woody plants root from stems if
they touch the soil for long enough (the basis of propagation
by layering), but few do it in the normal course of events.

Brambles are one of the exceptions, which explains why they are so good at tripping you up.

Runners, or stolons, are stems that creep along the ground, rooting at intervals. A single plant can form a large colony amazingly quickly; one white clover plant can produce up to 160 feet (50 meters) of stolons in a year. The only consolation is that you can at least see where they're going.

Rhizomes The weeds that really cause sleepless nights do their spreading below ground, more often than not by

Left to right: **Rampant roots include** bramble rooting stems; buttercup runners; ground-elder rhizomes; dock and dandelion taproots.

subterranean stems known as rhizomes. Rhizomes may travel great distances at considerable depth, making control (and even predicting where the plant will pop up next) extremely difficult. Horsetail rhizomes can travel up to 328 feet (100 meters) at a depth of up to 16 feet (5 meters). Most of these weeds can regenerate from fragments of rhizome that are tiny but usually much bigger than seeds, giving each new plant a formidable head start. Few weeds spread below ground by roots, but fireweed and creeping thistle are two of the exceptions.

Taproots Even roots that stay in the same place can make weeds hard to control. Dandelions and docks are just two common weeds with deep taproots. The temptation just to break off the plant near the surface is strong, but unless the whole root is removed, it will simply regrow. In fact, like the mythical Hydra (a nine-headed monster), the result is often more heads or weeds than you started with.

Bulbils Some of our most frustrating weeds, including lesser celandine (*Ranunculus ficaria*) and pink-flowered oxalis, form bulbs, bulbils, or tubers that break off when the plants are pulled up. Yellow nutsedge, a bad weed in regions with hot summers, has tubers *and* rhizomes—one tuber can become 6,900 in a single season. The fact that the tubers are edible is scant consolation.

Pink oxalis is also called
pink shamrock, but can
hardly be said
to be lucky—
each tiny bulbil
is a potential weed

Special mentions

In some ways, all weeds are the same (they all grow fast), but some are special cases. One example is lawn weeds, few of which cause much trouble elsewhere in the garden.

A PAIN IN THE GRASS

Any plant that lives in a lawn has to put up with being mowed every week. A few are genuinely tolerant of mowing, but most are basically flat.

Grass leaves grow from the plant bases, so mowing doesn't harm them, any more than trimming your hair or fingernails hurts you. They evolved this clever trick to deal with grazing animals, but it works just as well with mowers.

Many lawns start out from seed, others from turf, but in the end it doesn't make much difference. Just starting with a patch of bare earth and mowing whatever comes up has much the same result: a mix of grasses. In a UK survey of Sheffield lawns, "weed" grasses such as creeping bent, Yorkshire fog (*Holcus lanatus*), rough meadow grass (*Poa trivialis*), and annual meadow grass were nearly as abundant as the lawn grasses that are commonly sown. Indeed, rough meadow grass was the only grass—and only plant—present in every lawn we looked at.

Staying flat to avoid the mower blades is the strategy adopted by dandelions, plantains, and daisies—all classic lawn weeds. Daisies can be regarded as the most perfectly adapted, since not only the leaves but at least some of the short, leafless flower stems creep under the blades, so daisies can actually produce seeds in lawns.

Dandelion flowering stems are generally too tall to do this, so get mowed off. This means the dandelions in your lawn actually came (as seeds) from somewhere else. At the opposite extreme are plants like ragwort. This can survive for years as a vegetative rosette, but its flowering stem is tall and leafy, so ragwort plants in lawns never get to seed.

Short and creeping is the final weed strategy, adopted by some of the most abundant—and difficult to control—lawn weeds, including creeping buttercup, several speedwells, white clover, and lesser trefoil. Some weeds have combined creeping with another strategy, such as creeping bent and mouse-eared hawkweed (*Pilosella officinarum*), which has flat rosettes connected by creeping stems. All the common lawn mosses are also creeping.

WET AND WEEDY

Water weeds are another special case. Of course, you won't have genuinely aquatic weeds at all unless you have a pond and they can't escape into the rest of the garden. Almost all bad aquatic weeds, including fairy moss, floating pennywort, New Zealand pigmyweed, and parrot feather, are out-of-control ornamentals.

Removing any of these from a small pond shouldn't be too difficult, although the best approach is not to acquire them in the first place. In fact, none of them should be on sale any longer, so the chief danger is accepting a bucket of weed from a misguided friend. All these weeds can cause

big problems

if they escape into lakes and waterways, so, if you do have them, be very careful where you dispose of them.

Many native water plants, such as common reed (*Phragmites australis*) and white water lily are simply too large for the typical, small garden pond. You'll be forever cutting these down and pulling them out, so it is best not to plant them in the first place. Another native that can be very annoying is duckweed. You can try to stop it from ever arriving, but in my experience it usually gets you in the end.

I find a child's rake ideal for pulling algae and duckweed out of a small pond.

Friend or foe?

Gardeners are in general agreement about some weeds, but the frontier between weed and desirable garden plant is a disputed one. Follow the latest fashion or plow your own furrow? The choice is yours.

TOO MUCH OF A GOOD THING

The weeds mentioned so far are uninvited guests, but many so-called garden plants cause just as much trouble. Even the unmitigated thug Japanese knotweed started out as a prized ornamental, as did giant hogweed, ornamental jewelweed, and *Rhododendron ponticum*.

None of these is likely to cause much trouble in new gardens, if only because few gardeners would think of growing them. However, there are plenty of garden plants that some gardeners soon wish that they had never set eyes on. My own pet peeves among the prolific self-seeders are Welsh poppy and Spanish bluebell (*Hyacinthoides hispanica*). Spanish bluebell and I have fought each other to a standstill in my garden; the best thing I can say about my 10-year war of attrition is that there is no more of it now than when I started. The difficulty with these (and many others) is that their flowers are pretty, but unless you deadhead with ruthless efficiency, you will never stop them from seeding.

Among garden plants with vigorous vegetative reproduction, there are too many troublemakers to mention. One problem is that much depends on local circumstances of soil and climate, so that a plant that is a perfect monster in one place may be quite well-behaved (or even struggle to survive at all) in another.

Sterile spreaders Some weedy garden plants don't seed at all, but that doesn't seem to slow them down; instead, it merely allows them to concentrate on growing even faster. They include coppertip (*Crocosmia* x *crocosmiiflora*) and slender speedwell (*Veronica filiformis*).

Other garden thugs Abraham-Isaac-Jacob (*Trachystemon orientalis*), Peruvian lily (*Alstroemeria aurea*), several bamboos including *Sasa palmata* and *Sasaella ramosa*, the pink-flowered form of kaffir lily (*Schizostylis coccinea*), coltsfoot (*Tussilago farfara*), cypress spurge (*Euphorbia cyparissias*), and lemon balm (*Melissa officinalis*).

But don't regard this as a complete list, it is merely a short selection from a much longer one.

FICKLE FASHIONS

Gardening is as prone to the whims of fashion as any other human activity. When I was young, grass was something that belonged in the lawn. The only grudging exception might have been pampas grass (*Cortaderia selloana*), a plant so huge that it hardly seemed a grass at all. Had I predicted 40 years ago that tufted hair grass (*Deschampsia cespitosa*) and purple moor grass, native British plants that freely

Purple moor grass (*Molinia caerulea*)

grow wild in boggy countryside, would one day be sold as garden plants for a not-inconsiderable sum, I would have been assumed to have been at the *vino*.

Yet that curious state of affairs has indeed come to pass, and the *RHS Plant Finder* now lists plenty of suppliers of both in the UK. Had either plant, in those distant times, presumed to appear uninvited in the rose bed, it would have been instantly exterminated (had it even been recognized, which it almost certainly would not). Which is just by way of emphasizing that:

- weeds are plants you don't like (or haven't learned to like)
- even plants you *do* like can become weeds if they show any signs of making themselves too much at home.

There's nothing fundamentally unattractive about dandelions or hedge bindweed—I dare say that if they were difficult to grow, much effort would be expended in cultivating them, rather than in the merciless persecution they currently receive. Who can tell which weeds are just about to have their reputations rehabilitated by a change in taste?

In a recent magazine article, a correspondent was chortling with glee over his success in growing ivy broomrape (*Orobanche hederae*) in his garden. I don't mean to suggest that it is a weed, or in danger of becoming one, but if this leafless brown parasite becomes popular, maybe there's hope even for field horsetail?

KNOW YOUR SEEDLINGS

Many weeds start out as seedlings, and while you're happily hoeing away in the borders or the vegetable plot, it's easy to assume that all seedlings are bad news. As of course most of them are—but not all. To quote the great Christopher Lloyd, in his book *The Well-Tempered Garden*:

> I never like to weed out anything that I can't identify. Not all seedlings are weeds. You may feel that life is too short to leave a seedling in till it's large enough to identify. My own feeling is that life's too interesting not to leave it there until you can identify it. Taking this view, you will very soon learn to recognize weed seedlings when they are no larger than a pair of seed leaves. The not so easily identified ones will then most probably turn out to be the progeny of some of your border plants or shrubs, and it may suit you to save and grow them on.

You may not want to go as far as that, but if you are sowing seeds, either of crop plants or of ornamentals, it pays to have at least some idea what the resulting seedlings are supposed to look like.

If you are daunted by the task of identifying seedlings, location can be a useful guide. I've never noticed any seeds on my giant feather grass (*Stipa gigantea*), but weeding around it one day I noticed a grass seedling that looked a bit odd and decided to leave it. It turned out to be a *Stipa* seedling and has now grown into a handsome plant. I didn't want another plant—I hardly have room for the one I have—but I was able to give it to a friend, and very pleased he is with it, too.

You never know what might turn up. A study of seeds in the soil of Sheffield gardens, by collecting some small samples of soil and germinating the seeds in them, revealed (among many others) seeds of whiteweed, escallonias, fuchsias, and alumroot, as well as of *Lychnis coronaria* and *Verbena bonariensis*.

Seedlings worth saving in this patch include columbine (*bottom left*), foxgloves, and a tiny yew (*bottom right*).

TO WEED OR NOT TO WEED?

If asked why weeds deserve to be persecuted, I suspect most gardeners would offer as an excuse the weeds' interference with the growth of our crop plants and ornamentals. Many weeds certainly do that, and a few also act as hosts for pests or diseases that attack garden plants. But if that's all there is to it, why do so many gardeners take such exception to plants like lesser celandine?

I know gardeners who are incensed by the presence of celandine in their flower beds and devote a lot of time to trying to dig it up. Since it spreads by numerous, tiny bulbils, such efforts are nearly always in vain and may even result in spreading it around. But why bother? Celandine is not only small, it's the most fleeting of vernal ephemerals; by the time most garden plants are properly underway, celandine has disappeared until next spring. In short, celandine couldn't fight its way out of a paper bag and certainly is not equipped to do any real damage. It's also quite a welcome splash of color in early spring.

All that is required is some fairly minor rearrangement of one's mental furniture, and celandine ceases to be a problem. Recognizing that fact frees you from fighting a losing battle.

Lesser celandine (*Ranunculus ficaria*) is one of the first signs that winter is nearly over.

Of course, it's easy for me to say that—I don't have celandine in my garden. The thale cress in my vegetable plot is the most feeble of weeds, but I justify my persecution of it on the grounds that it gets hoed up along with other weeds that really are a problem.

Nothing brings out one's irrational hatred of a plant in the wrong place like lawns. I'm just grateful if my lawn stays green. I don't inquire too closely into what the green is made of—in my case, mostly moss, at least in winter. I also like many creeping lawn weeds, such as clover and speedwells; after all, what is a weedy lawn except a very short wildflower meadow?

Nor can I see much point in getting excited about "weed" grasses. No doubt lawn fanatics will soon be able to buy "Roundup Ready" red fescue and brown bent lawn grasses, thus allowing them to nuke all other plants, including the wrong sort of grass. If so, enjoy it while it lasts, because

weeds will have the
last laugh.

Indeed, the cat is already out of the bag. Golf greenskeepers are fond of creeping bent, which makes an excellent putting surface but is considered a weed in many lawns. They recently trialed a genetically modified, glyphosate-resistant variety in Oregon. It worked fine, except of course it escaped in the way GM plants always do. Oregon may be far away, but in time an indestructible version of this grass is coming to a lawn near you.

Love thine enemy?

Optimistic gardeners (or perhaps just lazy ones) are always on the lookout for uses for weeds, perhaps mindful of the old joke that a weed is "a plant whose virtues have yet to be discovered." So, are weeds any use?

Well, quite a few are considered to be edible. Chickweed, fat hen (*Chenopodium album*), goosegrass, ground-elder, and nettles have all been cooked like spinach at one time or another. Indeed, ground-elder was originally imported into Britain by the Romans as a vegetable, although its popularity was soon extinguished by its uncontrollable behavior. As long ago as the sixteenth century, John Gerard (in his famous *Herball*) was clearly fed up with ground-elder, describing it as

spoiling and getting every yeere more ground, to the annoying of better herbes.

Chickweed is also recommended as a salad ingredient, as is dandelion, which is hardly surprising since it's quite closely related to lettuce. Wild or prickly lettuce (*Lactuca virosa* and *L. serriola*) are quite common weeds in milder areas. Leaves of the wild lettuces, of dandelion, and of many of its weedy relatives (cat's-ear, nipplewort, rough hawkbit, and sowthistle) can all be added to salads. Young leaves are best; better still, blanch by earthing up or upending a pot over the plant, as you would if forcing rhubarb, before it produces a flower stem.

Are weeds worth growing to eat?

Well, I can't speak from experience, but when Richard Mabey in *Food for Free* describes ground-elder as "tangy and unusual" and dandelion as "pleasantly bracing," I'm sure he's trying to tell me something. Surely he could choose more alluring descriptions for plants he wanted to persuade me to eat. Eating weeds may give you a satisfying feeling of getting your own back, but there's always something more deserving that could occupy the same space. In a spirit of scientific inquiry, I recently had a nibble at some thale cress and it really isn't at all bad. But how much space would I have to devote to growing enough even for a single sandwich?

What of using weeds as a green manure? Most garden soils would benefit from more organic matter and few gardeners make enough of their own compost, so green manures have become a popular way of making up the deficit.

Popular green manures Buckwheat, clover, fenugreek, field beans, grazing rye, mustard, phacelia, and garden vetch—in fact, almost anything will do.

The idea is to grow something on soil that would otherwise be empty, and at some point cut it down and dig it into the soil or just allow it to rot. As well as adding organic matter, green manures protect the soil from rain and conserve nutrients. Green manures are usually grown from seed.

Since you tend to use green manure seeds in large quantities, and the cost is a major concern, it's tempting to see a good crop of annual weeds (*as below*) as a cheap alternative. However, the closer you look, the less attractive the prospect seems.

The ideal green manure is easily killed when the time comes; this can even be done for you since a tender crop such as buckwheat, fenugreek, or phacelia will be killed by the first hard

frost. The trouble with weeds is that they might be quite hard to kill when you want to; also, the large seed bank that they create will make weed control harder in the future. Ironically, one effect of a deliberately sown green manure is to *suppress* weeds.

Companion planting, another common practice, is based on the theory that growing other plants among vegetables helps to confuse insect pests and stop them from attacking crops. Smelly plants like garlic or marigolds are thought to do this best, but recent research shows that any plant will do, and that weeds are as good as anything else. Crops in weedy plots suffer less from pests than those in clean, weed-free soil, but there's a downside.

Weeds really do reduce plant growth by competing for space, water, and nutrients,

and it doesn't take many weeds to do this, especially when the crop plants are young. Companion planting is an excellent organic weapon against insect pests, but perhaps the best way to employ it is to mix up your vegetable plants and even throw in a few flowers, too, cottage-garden style.

To sum up, a common thread connects weeds as food, green manure, or companion plants: Yes, they can make a fair stab at all of them, but in every case there are better options. The best we can say is: If your weeds are out of control, it's not all bad news.

Weeding them out
Dig, hoe, and mulch

Weed all about it

Before we get down to the nitty gritty of how to control weeds, a few general points—about weedkillers, our attitude to weed problems, and avoiding trouble in the first place.

A WORD ABOUT WEEDKILLERS

You could, of course, kill your weeds with herbicide. At least, you can try. Indeed, it would be a brave organic gardener who could claim, when faced with bindweed or horsetail, never to have considered resorting to weedkillers.

Matthew Wilson contrasts his training, involving "chemical control and intervention in the pursuit of perfection," with the principle he now tries to follow: "Gardening is one 'can do' activity that can help us to lead more sustainable lives." Yet even he admits to finding it impossible, in his earlier role as curator of a Royal Horticultural Society garden, to survive without glyphosate.

This is the last time I'm going to mention herbicides in this book. Not because I disapprove; if you want to use herbicides, I trust you to buy the right chemical for the job, read the label, and

use it safely. But herbicides are costly and may be damaging to the wider environment; the range of chemicals available to gardeners decreases every year; and more and more gardeners would like to manage without them. The increasing use of crops that have been genetically modified to be resistant to herbicides has resulted in more herbicide-resistant weeds. We can now take advantage of the innovative methods being developed to help organic farmers deal with weeds without chemicals. So,

onward
and **upward,**
to a **chemical-free future!**

TRUCE OR TOTAL WAR?

Old hippies may not like this, but there really is no way of arriving at a *modus vivendi* with weeds. The phrase "give them an inch and they'll take a mile" sums it up perfectly. Ignore a small weed problem and it will become a large one. For anyone who is serious about weed control, the ultimate aim should be to reduce the problem to a level where further control requires relatively little effort.

Does this mean that you should aim for eradication? Well, maybe, sometimes. The more serious perennial weeds are so troublesome that I think

total eradication
should be your ultimate aim.

I inherited a fair amount of creeping thistle when I bought my present house, but a zero-tolerance approach over several years paid dividends and it's now extinct—in my garden, anyway.

The good thing about most perennial weeds is that they don't produce many seeds, and the few they do produce are not widely dispersed—so if you can eliminate them, they are unlikely to return. Nevertheless, be realistic. There are many weeds—the majority—where eradication is not possible.

You will never remove all trace of weeds that can seed prolifically, such as dandelions and willowherbs, or those whose seeds persist in the soil. No dock plant has survived long enough to set seed since I moved into my present home 18 years ago, but I'm still digging up dock seedlings. On a timescale relevant to gardeners, many weed seeds are effectively immortal. The best you can hope for is to stop your weeds adding to the seed bank in the soil; if you do that well enough, the problem of continually emerging weeds will—slowly—decline.

Ask yourself how much you care about weeds and how much time and energy you are prepared to put into controlling them.

- If the answer to both questions is "a lot," you should get on top of your weeds eventually.
- If both answers are "not much," that's OK too; your weeds will get the upper hand, but relax—you don't care!
- The worst case scenario—and I fear the one that afflicts many gardeners—is to be anxious about weeds, but lack any serious intention to do anything about them.

Whatever kind of gardener you are, I hope to show you that all is not lost and that

weeds are
not as invincible
as you thought.

DON'T INHERIT TROUBLE

Of course, you would never let a weed problem get completely out of control, but there are plenty of careless people out there who would. The story of the people who moved to a new house to escape pink oxalis may be apocryphal, but, if it's true, do you want to be the mug who inherited their garden?

When buying a new house, try to make sure that you see the garden in summer, when any serious weed problem should be obvious. Personally, I would regard a garden overgrown by ground-elder or Japanese knotweed as at least as good grounds for haggling over the price as, say, rotten window frames or leaking gutters—in fact, better grounds, because the latter problems are more easily fixed.

If perennial weeds like ground-elder are sneaking under the fence from next door, you need a serious talk with your neighbor.

DON'T IMPORT TROUBLE

The weeds you already have are bad enough. You don't want any more. So your first priority is not to buy any garden plants that will become weeds. For example, as I've already mentioned, Spanish bluebell and I have been locked in mortal combat for over 10 years, but according to the *RHS Plant Finder*, there are still several nurseries out there that would be happy to sell me some more.

Personally, I think you would have to be crazy to grow it, but, if you must, all you have to do is wait until a friend is throwing out a bucketful. Then at least you can later reflect that the source of your misfortunes didn't actually cost you anything.

But, you might reasonably ask, how am I supposed to know what these evil plants are *before* I plant them? Well, there are several giveaway signs. If a friend offers you a clump of, say, variegated yellow archangel (*Lamium galeobdolon* subsp. *montanum* 'Florentinum'), ask yourself why he has it to spare.

Read catalog descriptions carefully for warning signs. For example, one nursery offers the plant with this description:

"...one of the easiest solutions to dry shade areas. Plants form a **fast-spreading**, bushy carpet of attractive, green and silver leaves, bearing small, soft-yellow flowers in mid-spring...Stems **root into the ground readily, where they touch**. It has an **aggressive habit**, but this is not a problem unless unleashed into the border...**Easily increased** by moving rooted plantlets in spring or fall."

This particular nursery obviously has a slight conscience about selling you such a thug, so they even go as far as "aggressive," although hastily adding that this is "not a problem." Here are some other catalog descriptions of the same plant:

"Spreads quickly from long runners. A rampant grower for problem areas..."

"Does not tolerate other plants well..."

"Some say that Yellow Archangel is somewhat invasive."

"Useful for covering areas in the dry shade where little else will grow. Has fast-growing, long branches."

"Excellent, aggressive ground cover with silver-variegated leaves. Will cover large areas under trees."

"Spreading habit—great ground cover for problem shady areas."

Do you begin to
see a pattern here?

I like the tortured attempts to persuade you to buy, while hinting that this is a plant that you do not want. "Does not tolerate other plants well" is practically a dictionary definition of a weed. Others try to be honest, even though they can't quite bring themselves to admit the horrible truth, as in "Some say that Yellow Archangel is somewhat invasive." My favorite nursery even has a category for such plants, calling them "Wicked Ruggeds (perennials that last the test of time, rugged, hardy and durable)." In other words,

you have been
warned.

Even if the plant you're buying is harmless, that's far from the end of your problems. Inspect plants in garden centers carefully before buying: willowherbs and hairy bittercress are among the commonest weeds of container-grown plants. The former is too well dispersed to be avoided, but if you're one of the lucky few who don't have hairy bittercress, you don't want to import it. Even if it is not actually growing in the pot with the plant you want, check if there is a lot of it around the nursery. If there is, its seeds are almost certainly in the pot somewhere.

There may even be roots or rhizomes of perennial weeds lurking in the compost. One acquaintance accidentally introduced a small piece of ground-elder with a plant from a nursery, and has spent the last 10 years trying to get rid of it.

Tools of the trade

Some tools, such as the spade and fork, are used for various jobs in the garden, including weeding. For digging up weeds, the smaller (border) version of both is the most useful. A small hand fork is also an essential tool for those who like to get down and dirty with their weeds and those who want to spare self-sown seedlings of garden plants. There are also other more exotic weeding tools, such as flame weeders.

The single most useful weeding tool is the hoe, used to control weeds between plants in beds or in the vegetable plot. There are several types of hoe, and tool manufacturers keep inventing new ones. Of the two most common types, the draw hoe is designed to be used with a downward chopping motion, while the scuffle hoe has a cutting edge at the front that slides along just below the soil surface. For those with large gardens or back problems, a wheel hoe may be a worthwhile investment.

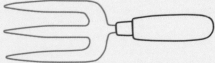

Clockwise from top left: **Weeding tools** include the wheel hoe, draw hoe, and hand fork.

Use whichever hoe suits you, but whatever you choose, the rules are the same:

- Keep the blade clean and sharp—remember, you want to decapitate the weeds, not just rough them up a bit.
- Use the hoe when the soil surface is dry, so that severed or uprooted weeds die quickly. Anything else that speeds up drying out will also help—good weather for line-drying laundry is good weather for hoeing. Nevertheless, don't abandon hoeing in the face of a prolonged spell of wet weather; hoe anyway, then rake up the weeds and put them on the compost heap.
- Do not let weeds get out of hand; the smaller they are, the easier they are to kill. If you hoe when you notice the first weed seedlings, you will also kill all those you haven't noticed yet.
- Remember, it's a hoe, not a small spade. The blade should slide along just below the soil surface. A hoe is most effective if it chops weeds exactly into roots and shoots.
- Regular use of the hoe every two weeks will control annual weeds and seedlings of perennial weeds, but there are much better ways of dealing with established perennial weeds (*see pages 72–79*).

A **scuffle hoe** is the original and still the best.

PREVENTION OR CURE?

Killing weed seedlings is not too difficult, but ideally one would like to prevent them from germinating in the first place. Weed seeds are not stupid: They are programmed to germinate where there is plenty of space, water, light, and nutrients. Deny them these things and most of them will fail to germinate.

Mulch vs. weeds Bare ground (*left*) is an easy win for weeds; a loose mulch (*center*) will hold back most weeds, but for total victory, you need weed-suppressing membrane (*right*); cover it with ornamental mulch if you wish.

Therefore, the first line of defense is a good, dense cover of garden plants. If you're happy with a layer of ground-cover plants, you will find that they will do most of your weed control for you.

Good ground cover *Cotoneaster dammeri*, epimediums, winter creeper, geraniums, heathers, trailing hebes, *Lamium maculatum*, and lesser periwinkle (*Vinca minor*).

You can cover bare soil between plants with a mulch of at least 4 inches (10 centimeters) of garden compost, leaf mold, bark, shredded prunings, or wood chips. More unusual mulches, such as sawdust from a local sawmill or spent hops from a brewery, may be available cheaply in your neighborhood. For added insurance, lay the mulch on top of a layer of wet newspaper or cardboard.

The mulch will drastically reduce the amount of weeding you need to do, although you will still need to watch for weeds that blow in on the wind. Remember to top up the layer of mulch occasionally. An added benefit of this approach is that the mulch will gradually decay, improving soil structure as it does so. Some garden books tell you that these organic mulches will rob your soil of nitrogen as they decay, but

this problem is greatly exaggerated.

A combination of dense planting and mulching suppresses most annual and some perennial weeds in permanent beds or borders, but there are parts of the garden where bare ground cannot be avoided. Chief among these is the vegetable plot, but similar problems occur if you grow a lot of annual bedding plants.

Here is where frequent use of a sharp hoe really comes into its own. Some people think hoeing is the worst form of drudgery, but there are plenty of things you can do to make it easier.

Make a stale seedbed (*see pages 66–67*).

Soil solarization is a clever variation on the stale
seedbed. Cover the bare soil with clear plastic for at least six weeks in the summer so the surface soil gets hot, which kills weed seeds and some pathogens, too. The soil must be

moist, so if it's dry, water it first. This technique works a whole lot better in regions that have hot summers with plenty of sunshine.

Start seeds under glass Many gardeners have trouble distinguishing weed seedlings from crop seedlings. Not only that, weeds compete very effectively with crops (or bedding plants) if they emerge at the same time.

One way around this is to raise crop seedlings in small modules in a cold frame or greenhouse, or even on a windowsill, and then plant them out. This way, you can continue hoeing the entire bed right up until you plant, the crop plants are large and obvious, and they get a head start on any late-germinating weeds.

Sow in rows Think carefully about how you grow the crop. Many books recommend broadcast sowing direct-sown crops like carrots (rather than sowing in rows), on the grounds that it makes better use of the available space. Maybe it does, but it makes it harder to distinguish crop seedlings from weed seedlings and makes weeding much trickier. Weeding between rows is easy with a hoe—only weeds actually within the rows require tedious hand weeding.

Sow in a grid To make hoeing even easier, you could grow some crops, such as onions, carrots, or radishes, in small clusters, with little or no effect on yield. If the clusters are sown in a grid pattern, the normal distinction between "within rows" and "between rows" disappears; you can then hoe easily in both directions, virtually eliminating the need for hand weeding.

Hand weed Once weeds are mostly under control, it's not difficult to keep it that way by hand weeding. Most annual weeds, and perennial seedlings, are easily pulled up, especially from moist soil. If you pull young weeds as you stroll around the garden (carry a hand fork if you don't want to get your hands dirty), they'll never be a big problem.

Never lose sight of what you're trying to achieve. Your primary goal is to stop weeds from interfering with the growth of your plants. Transplanting well-grown plants into a clean seedbed will do that fairly well; such plants often shrug off competition from late-germinating weeds. An important secondary aim is to reduce future trouble by preventing weeds from seeding; even weeds too small to affect a crop may still produce lots of seeds.

Always kill weeds before they can seed.

Hoeing is a breeze if you sow in a grid pattern.

STALE SEEDBED

The idea of a stale (or false) seedbed is to cultivate the soil a few weeks before you plan to sow, which stimulates a crop of weed seedlings. You can then kill these seedlings just before sowing.

- **Clear all weeds** from the plot, digging out any roots or rhizomes, and roughly level the soil.

- **Rake the soil** to a fine tilth and leave for 3–4 weeks, until a new crop of weeds appears.

- **Hoe the weed seedlings** as lightly and with as little soil disturbance as possible, to avoid stimulating germination of yet more weeds. Luckily, even very little disturbance will kill seedlings with only 2–4 leaves.

- **Alternatively, use a flame weeder**, which doesn't disturb the soil at all. You can continue to use a flame weeder even after sowing, as long as you stop before the crop seedlings come through. Remember: Very small weeds are killed much more easily than larger ones; a single pass with the flame is enough—you do not need to burn the weeds to a crisp; a flame weeder works best on dry weeds and soil.

Mowing them down

I wish there were an easy organic treatment for lawn weeds, but there isn't. Lawns are only a domesticated version of pasture, and pastures are naturally full of lots of different plants, many of them not grasses, so why should lawns be any different?

Experience suggests that many gardeners know that a weed-free lawn is more trouble than it's worth. In a survey of more than 50 garden lawns, we found that the average lawn contained 24 different kinds of plants, of which most were not grasses. No lawn consisted only of grass; there were dandelions in every lawn we looked at, except one. So, if you have weeds in your lawn, at least you are not alone! When it comes to lawn weeds, prevention is much better than cure. To control them, you can:

Avoid walking on your lawn when it's very wet or dry or frozen. Weeds invade bare, worn patches. Don't allow wear in one place; move around equipment such as garden furniture and children's swings.

Feed your lawn and mow frequently—lawns with vigorous grass have fewer weeds. Do not set the mower blades too low and keep them sharp. The worst thing you can do is to try to economize on mowing by letting the lawn grow too long and then "scalping" the grass.

In dry spells, don't water (or feed) your lawn. It's a waste of water and will encourage some weeds.

Rake before mowing to raise up the stems of creeping weeds and allow the mower to cut them off.

Increase the soil acidity by regularly applying ammonium-sulphate fertilizer. (A neutral or alkaline soil encourages most lawn weeds.) Acidic soil also deters earthworms, which means fewer unsightly worm casts to act as focal points for weed invasion.

Keep the lawn well drained and avoid shade to minimize moss, which likes it damp and cool.

Dig out individual weeds such as daisies with a knife, hand fork, or special weeding tool. Fill each hole with soil and top with grass seed. Slash unsightly weed grasses with a sharp knife before mowing—control can take time.

If reading all that makes you want to lie down in the shade with a stiff drink, maybe you should just learn to enjoy your lawn weeds.

A rock and a hard place

Some gardeners are driven to distraction by weeds of hard surfaces; even frequently applying (costly) weedkillers may not offer a complete solution. Traditionally, weeds are removed from gaps in paving with a special hooked knife, but you could use a wire brush.

Regular brushing with a good, stiff yard brush can help control weeds, and also removes the dust, mud, and plant debris that promote weed germination and growth. Another option is to blast the weeds out of paving cracks with a high-pressure washer. However, these methods are hard work and not totally effective, nor can they be used on gravel. The best solution for gravel is to lay it on a permeable membrane, to prevent weeds from rooting into the soil and make them easy to deal with. Of course, this doesn't help if you already have gravel directly on the soil.

Flame-weeding is probably the best all-purpose weed control method for both paving and gravel; it's most effective on young weeds and on a dry day. Large parts of individual weeds may be relatively inaccessible, in deep cracks or buried in gravel, which reduces the efficacy of the treatment, so be prepared for some weeds to survive and to have to repeat the treatment.

Perennial problem

There is no easy solution to perennial weeds, but you can make your life slightly easier by containing the problem. Assuming that the bindweed or whatever is confined to part of your garden, you should make strenuous efforts to make sure that it stays there. Do not inadvertently move it around with other plants, or in soil or compost.

I'm constantly amazed by how widespread Japanese knotweed is in the UK, since it does not seed in the country and so can be moved from one garden to another only in soil. You can compost roots or rhizomes of perennial weeds safely, but make very sure that they are dead first: bake them; drown them in a bucket of water for at least six weeks; or beat them to a pulp with a hammer.

Another priority is speed. The worst perennial weeds can spread over yards in one season, so **the time to act is now.**

A small weed infestation is easier to deal with than a large one: however big the problem is this year, next year it will be bigger.

Bake perennial weeds in the sun until they look like vampires in the final scene of *Dracula*

Cultivate such virtues as determination, persistence, thoroughness, and—especially unfashionable these days—patience. Neglecting perennial weeds for long periods, then going at them like a bull in a china shop achieves nothing. Digging them into the soil or rotavating the whole area generally makes it worse—every bit of root or rhizome will grow into a new plant.

Hoeing, if done often and thoroughly, will suppress the weeds, but not kill them. It's really only useful in bare ground; among flowers and shrubs, where perennial weeds are usually a problem, hoeing is rarely an option. Pulling up shoots when you see them also won't kill the weeds and you will always miss shoots. Digging out as much root as you can works better, but again is almost impossible where weeds mix with shrubs or herbaceous plants.

The only long-term solution is to remove everything—garden plants and weeds—from a bed or border and start again with clean soil. Dig up all the ornamentals you want to save, carefully remove all traces of weed root and rhizome from among their roots, and temporarily replant elsewhere. To eliminate weeds from the bed, you have essentially two options.

You can wait and thoroughly dig out every piece of weed root and rhizome as soon as you see any growth above ground (digging through the soil to find bits of rhizome before they grow is just impossible). Alternatively, simply cover the soil with a tough layer (old carpet or newspapers are perfect) to prevent weed growth, and wait for the weeds to die. Whichever method you choose, be patient; complete control will take at least a year, probably more.

BARRIER METHOD

Once the soil is clean, you can replant your weed-free plants. To eliminate future weeding, cover the bed with a permeable, weed-suppressing membrane.

Woven polypropylene weed-suppressing, or landscape, fabric is ideal, but old carpet is a cheap alternative. Black plastic is sometimes recommended, but it prevents water from reaching the soil and is not a long-term solution. Do not be tempted to cut corners by laying the anti-weed membrane over an existing perennial weed problem. The weeds will find a way out through

To plant through a membrane: cut a cross; fold back the flaps; dig out some soil; insert a plant; firm; water; replace the flaps and mulch; repeat as needed.

the planting holes and the more vigorous weeds will even come through the membrane (Japanese knotweed, horsetail, and even dandelions quite happily grow through tarmac).

Before laying the membrane, cultivate and level the soil. Plant your garden plants individually through small holes cut in the membrane. It doesn't look very nice, so cover it with gravel or slate chippings or a good layer of compost, wood chips, or bark. You can then easily pull up any weed seedlings that appear.

COVER-UP

A weed-suppressing membrane is not to everyone's taste, so if you're absolutely sure that all traces of perennial weeds have been removed, you could make do with a thick layer—at least 4 inches (10 cm)—of just compost or bark. Such a thick mulch will stop weed seedlings emerging from the soil, although you will still need to pull up seedlings of dandelions and willowherbs that blow in from elsewhere.

But you must first have cleared 100 percent of the existing perennial weeds—no amount of organic mulch is any defense against them. Dense planting will also help to prevent new weeds establishing from seeds in the soil bank.

Bare ground is an open **invitation to weeds.**

A thick bark mulch around *Hosta*.

Resistance will be futile

As the area under organic farming increases, the number of available weedkillers shrinks, and more and more weeds become resistant to herbicides, interest in novel methods of weed control grows. Much of the more exotic research is nearly always carried out by men who spent their youth playing with chemistry sets and trains; it involves high-voltage electricity, liquid nitrogen, UV light, microwaves, and lasers.

At this stage, **most** of the **equipment** is as dangerous to the operator as it is to weeds, **so don't hold your breath.**

The most promising avenue is to combine traditional physical control (essentially, hoeing) with recent developments in computing and artificial intelligence; in other words, robot weeders. To find out what the experts have been up to, look at the website (http://www.fieldrobotevent.de/) of an annual competition in robotic farming. (The contest was founded at Wageningen University, The Netherlands, and is now held in Germany.) At the very least, it will take your mind off worrying about your weeds.

International FieldRobotEvent 2008—the winner (*right*) and third-prize holder (*left*) of the Challenge event—weeding in a maize field.

Rogues' gallery: annuals Here today, still here tomorrow

ANNUAL MEADOW GRASS

We start our survey of annuals of temperate climates with perhaps the world's most ubiquitous weed. Annual meadow grass is the perfect plant with which to check if the lie-detector is working – anyone who says that they don't have it is fibbing. It is often considered a bad lawn weed and is hated by keepers of golf greens.

- **How it succeeds** It grows almost everywhere (in cultivated ground, paths, paving, lawns) and can germinate and flower at any time of year. The seeds persist in the soil and the life cycle is short (as little as 44 days). Its fibrous roots make it difficult to hoe or pull up; even if uprooted, it has remarkable powers of survival, especially in the wet.

- **What to do** Hoe at first sight; seedlings are much easier to kill than older plants. This weed's small size makes it unable to penetrate a mulch or dense planting.

- **Silver lining** Its ability to germinate at any time and tolerate shade, drought, soil compaction, and close mowing make it a surprisingly useful turf grass. A typical lawn is about two per cent annual meadow grass.

Annual meadow grass *Poa annua* ↕ 8 in (20 cm) ✿ all year

SCARLET PIMPERNEL

This low, spreading weed is also known as poor man's weatherglass, from its habit of closing its small, but vivid flowers in cloudy or wet weather. A form with blue flowers is common in warm climates.

- **How it succeeds** Scarlet pimpernel is happy in any open, sunny spot. Like most annual weeds, it is fast-growing and produces tiny seeds that can survive in the soil for decades.

- **What to do** Hoe or hand weed before it seeds. It is easily prevented from germinating by the cover of a mulch or established planting.

- **Silver lining** This annual weed is too small to cause a really serious problem, even if abundant, and it does have pretty flowers.

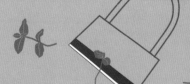

Scarlet pimpernel *Anagallis arvensis*
↕ 8 in (20 cm) ✿ early summer–early fall

CRESSES

Common in cultivated ground, this collection of small, unimpressive, mostly spring-flowering weeds all have white flowers that are so tiny they are almost invisible.

- **How they succeed** All have short life cycles, sometimes very short (as little as three weeks for thale cress), and small seeds that can survive in soil for decades. Hairy bittercress also has explosive seed capsules that fling seeds far and wide; it is an almost ubiquitous contaminant of container-grown plants in nurseries and garden centers.

- **What to do** To avoid trouble in future, it's crucial to prevent seeding. Hoe or hand weed, although swine cress is annoyingly difficult to pull up. You can easily prevent them from germinating with a mulch or established planting.

- **Silver lining** These relatives of cabbage and of watercress are all edible, although their small size and short life cycles mean that they never produce much that is worth eating.

Clockwise from top left: **swine cress** *Coronopus squamatus* ↕ 10 in (25 cm) ✿ summer–fall; **shepherd's purse** *Capsella bursa-pastoris* ↕ 20 in (50 cm) ✿ all year; **hairy bittercress** *Cardamine hirsuta* ↕ 12 in (30 cm) ✿ mid-spring–early fall; **thale cress** *Arabidopsis thaliana* ↕ 12 in (30 cm) ✿ mid-spring–early summer

SPEEDWELLS

Every family has a black sheep: among speedwells, the ivy-leaved form is it. Most speedwells have pretty blue flowers and many are grown as ornamentals, but the flowers of the ivy-leaved speedwell are so small and fleeting that you would hardly notice them.

- **How they succeed** Field speedwell (*Veronica persica*) can flower all year round, while ivy-leaved speedwell produces seeds very quickly in spring, before most gardeners notice the problem. Both are widespread in cultivated soil, where their seeds persist.

- **What to do** Both are shallow-rooted and prostrate, so are easily killed by hoeing or suppressed by mulch or dense plant cover. Ivy-leaved speedwell seedlings are conspicuous even when young, so look out for them in spring.

- **Did you know?** The speedwell that most commonly infests lawns is slender speedwell (*V. filiformis*), an escaped, former rock-garden plant.

Ivy-leaved speedwell *Veronica hederifolia* ↕ 12 in (30 cm) ✿ mid-spring–early summer. Inset: **germander speedwell** *V. chamaedrys* also frequents lawns.

KNOTGRASS

Despite its common name, knotgrass is – clearly – not a grass. In fact, it is a small, mostly prostrate weed that is an annual relative of Japanese knotweed (*see pages 140–41*).

- **How it succeeds** This weed is common in cultivated ground, gardens, and especially compacted soil by paths. Like most successful annual weeds, it combines rapid growth with large numbers of small, persistent seeds.

- **What to do** Hoeing while weeds are small is effective, but older plants develop taproots and regrow if the tops are cut off. Since knotgrass germinates only in spring, you will find no new seedlings after early summer. It is easily suppressed by a mulch or dense planting.

- **Did you know?** Knotgrass has a climbing relative, black bindweed (*Fallopia convolvulus*), which can be a bad weed and is sometimes mistaken for bindweed. It has the same tiny flowers as knotgrass, but larger, more bindweed-like leaves. Unlike true bindweed (*see pages 144–45*), it's an annual, so is much easier to control.

Knotgrass *Polygonum aviculare* ↕ 12 in (30 cm) ✿ mid-summer–late fall. Inset: **the flowers** are tiny.

SPURGES

Spurges all have tiny, greenish flowers surrounded by conspicuous bracts. These two weed species are annuals, but many perennial euphorbias are grown as garden plants; Robb's spurge (*E. amygdaloides* var. *robbiae*) can be rather invasive.

- **How they succeed** Both weed species thrive in any cultivated soil by means of rapid growth, short life cycles, and long-persistent seeds. They are easily overlooked even when flowering.

- **What to do** Hoe or hand weed. These weeds are easily suppressed by mulch or dense perennial planting.

- **Warning!** When damaged, all spurges exude a bitter, milky latex that causes skin irritation in some people, so wear gloves if hand weeding. The same warning applies to the perennial garden plants.

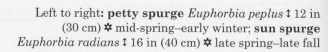

Left to right: **petty spurge** *Euphorbia peplus* ↕ 12 in (30 cm) ✿ mid-spring–early winter; **sun spurge** *Euphorbia radians* ↕ 16 in (40 cm) ✿ late spring–late fall

GROUNDSEL

Although it is a member of the daisy family, this is one of the least attractive; each "flower" (actually a collection of tiny, individual flowers) lacks the usual ring of large outer flowers, or "petals."

- **How it succeeds** Groundsel is very common in cultivated ground and gardens, on all soils, utilizing rapid growth, a short life cycle, and abundant seed production. Its seeds do not survive for many years in the soil, but are very effectively dispersed by wind. This weed can germinate and flower all year round.

- **What to do** Hoeing is effective, but as usual works better if the weeds are young. Hand pulling works too, but uprooted plants may survive (and produce seed), especially in damp weather. Small seedlings are easily suppressed by a mulch or dense planting.

- **Did you know?** Groundsel hybridized with the alien Oxford ragwort (*Senecio squalidus*) to give rise to Welsh groundsel (*Senecio cambrensis*), a new species and one of the UK's very few endemic plants.

Groundsel *Senecio vulgaris* ↕ 15 in (38 cm) ✿ all year.
Inset: **the seedling** is distinct once it has 4–6 leaves.

CHICKWEED

This rather limp, pale-green annual, with prostrate, spreading stems and small, white flowers, is a common weed across the world.

- **How it succeeds** Very common in rich, cultivated soil, chickweed grows very fast and can germinate, flower, and seed all year round. To top it all, its seeds persist in the soil for decades.

- **What to do** Hoeing is effective, but preferably when the plants are young and the weather is dry. It's easy and rather satisfying to pull up handfuls, but the stems are brittle and some is always left behind. The priority is to take action early and prevent seeding.

- **Silver lining** As the common name suggests, chickweed has a long history as food for chickens and caged birds. The plant is edible to humans too, raw or cooked, but it's difficult to collect enough, or to gather leaves without a mud garnish.

Chickweed *Stellaria media*
↕ 20 in (50 cm) ✿ all year

NIPPLEWORT

A tall member of the daisy family, this weed starts out as a rosette of leaves, but soon produces a tall, thin flower stem with numerous yellow flowers. The common name is supposed to derive from the shape of the flower buds.

- **How it succeeds** Nipplewort is common in gardens and cultivated land, but also in hedgerows and waste places. It grows fast and has persistent seeds, and its height allows it to compete with other tall plants.

- **What to do** Hoe it while it is young. Hand pulling is effective as long as you grasp each stem near the base. It takes a while to flower and is slow to shed its ripe seeds, so it's relatively easy to prevent it from seeding.

- **Silver lining** Like many dandelion relatives, it has edible young leaves.

Nipplewort *Lapsana communis*
↕ 38 in (95 cm) ✿ midsummer–mid-fall

COMMON SOWTHISTLE

Despite its name, common sowthistle isn't very thistle-like, but its annual relative, spiny sowthistle, has more spiny leaves. There is also a perennial sowthistle, *Sonchus arvensis*, which spreads by creeping roots. Like dandelions, all sowthistles release milky latex when damaged.

- **How it succeeds** Common in cultivated ground, gardens and waste places, these weeds thrive by rapid growth and abundant production (up to 18,000 per plant of prickly sowthistle) of very effectively wind-dispersed seeds.

- **What to do** Hoeing is effective, but hand pulling isn't, since the stems usually break at the base, leaving the taproots in the ground. All sowthistles grow moderately large before flowering, so there is time to prevent seeding.

- **Silver lining** Sowthistles, like dandelions, can be used as salad vegetables, although you need to trim the spines off more prickly species first. Theseus is supposed to have dined off sowthistle before sorting out the Minotaur, so they must be OK. Rabbits love them.

Clockwise from top left: **common sowthistle** *Sonchus oleraceus* ↕ 3–5 ft (90–150 cm) ✿ early summer–early fall, flowers and seedhead; **spiny sowthistle** *Sonchus asper* seedlings

GOOSEGRASS OR CLEAVERS

The stems and leaves of this plant stick to most kinds of clothing, which is why you threw handfuls of it at your friends when you were young.

- **How it succeeds** Common in fertile soils, it gets a head start by germinating in winter, while most gardeners are still dormant. Its large seeds and long, scrambling stems, both covered with hooked bristles, give it the ability to escape attention by growing up inside shrubs and hedges. The seeds hitch a ride on animal and human coats to travel great distances. Goosegrass also has the annoying habit of often growing along with nettles.

- **What to do** Goosegrass is easily killed by hoeing but, unusually for an annual, is difficult to pull up, because its brittle stems usually break. Since it grows into a large plant before flowering, there's plenty of time for alert gardeners to kill it before it seeds.

- **Silver lining** The nutrient-rich stems and leaves make good compost, if you can collect enough. It can be used as food for animals (including geese, as its common name suggests) and, if cooked like spinach, for humans too.

Goosegrass *Galium aparine* ↕ 6 ft (2 m) ✿ early summer–early fall

ORNAMENTAL JEWELWEED

This large annual weed is another of those plants that started out as a garden plant, but proved so troublesome that it is no longer grown.

- **How it succeeds** It likes any damp, fertile soil and will tolerate a fair amount of shade. Large seeds and extremely rapid growth allow it to compete even with vigorous perennials like nettles. The seed pods burst open when mature and scatter seeds across several yards.

- **What to do** Since it grows into a large plant before flowering, there's plenty of time to prevent it from seeding. It is easily controlled by hoeing young plants or by cutting it down before flowering, but can be a serious pest if you allow it to seed. There is only a single spring flush of seedlings and seeds do not persist in the soil.

- **Silver lining** Jewelweed flowers are a magnet for bees. The exploding seed pods are much enjoyed by children of all ages. The seeds and unripe fruits are (allegedly) edible.

Ornamental jewelweed *Impatiens glandulifera*
↕ 6 ft (2 m) ✿ midsummer–late fall

Warm-climate weeds

Most of the weeds in this book are at home in temperate regions, even if some of them come from warmer climates. But there are a few annuals that have yet to make much of an impact in such regions, but are common in areas that have warmer summers.

Most temperate weeds photosynthesize (make energy from sunlight) in the same way as most other plants, but amaranth and foxtails perform C4 photosynthesis. This works better in hot, dry climates, producing more sugar to fuel even faster growth.

Gallant soldier is an annual daisy of cultivated soil from South America, as is shaggy soldier (*Galinsoga quadriradiata*). They are very similar and effectively indistinguishable.

Both are hosts to several pests and diseases, including cucumber mosaic virus. They grow and flower very rapidly and can produce several generations in one year. Hoeing, hand pulling, and mulching are all effective. Their Achilles heels are relatively short-lived seeds, so you can eradicate them if you can prevent seeding for 3–4 years.

Cocklebur is a coarse, tall weed. Its chief claim to fame is its seeds, which are encased in burrs covered with hooked spines that often become entangled in animal hair; the burrs can reduce the value of sheep fleeces. It is related to ragweed and is another cause of hay fever. The seeds persist in the soil and the priority, as usual, is to prevent it from seeding.

Despite its bad reputation, however, cocklebur has a place in scientific history: It played a key role in the discovery of how plants flower in response to changing day length. Its burrs were also one of the inspirations for Velcro.

Left to right: **gallant soldier** *Galinsoga parviflora* ‡ 32 in (80 cm) ✿ late spring–late fall; **cocklebur** *Xanthium strumarium* ‡ 3 ft (1 m) ✿ late summer–mid-fall

Foxtail Yellow foxtail and bristly foxtail (*Setaria verticillata*) are fast-growing grasses that thrive in cultivated soil, waste places, and in arable crops. Bristly foxtail has barbed seeds and gets stuck in animal fur. Hoe, hand pull, and mulch; it's vital to stop seeding. There are several other, similar species.

Amaranth, also called pigweed, is one of many similar species. It germinates in summer and flowers and seeds rapidly. Seedlings grow slowly at first and are easily killed by hoeing. You can hand pull larger plants, but do it before they set seed—the abundant seeds persist in the soil.

Ragweed is the most significant cause of hay fever in eastern North America. Each plant produces one billion pollen grains—that's 100 million tons of pollen every year in North America. Ragweed grows very quickly, but it is a tall plant, so there's plenty of time to intervene and prevent it from flowering. The seeds persist for a long time in soil.

Ivy-leaf morning glory is a beautiful, tropical vine and is a popular garden plant in cooler climates, but in warmer climates, it grows all too quickly and seeds profusely. The key is to prevent it from seeding—or just enjoy it.

Clockwise from top left: **yellow foxtail** *Setaria glauca* ↕ 28 in (70 cm) ✿ mid–late summer; **amaranth** *Amaranthus hybridus* ↕ 3 ft (1 m) ✿ midsummer–mid-fall; **ragweed** *Ambrosia artemisiifolia* ↕ 3 ft (1 m) ✿ late summer–early fall; **ivy-leaf morning glory** *Ipomoea hederacea* ↕ 10 ft (3 m) ✿ early summer–mid-fall

Rogues' gallery: perennials Persistent, resistant, defiant

MOTHER OF THOUSANDS

A plant whose Latin name presumably reflects an ambition to get as close as possible to breaking the rule that genus and species names cannot be the same, without actually doing so. This native of Sardinia and Corsica was introduced as a rock-garden plant, although it's hard to see why.

- **How it succeeds** This weed forms a green carpet in damp, shady places, on walls, pavements, and lawns. The prostrate, creeping stems root at every node, so every tiny fragment is a potential new plant.

- **What to do** In damp, shady corners, mother of thousands doesn't really do any harm. It's the tendency to invade lawns that most annoys gardeners; it's resistant to all lawn weedkillers. You could try to remove small patches by hand, then resow with fresh grass. All the general advice about lawn weeds applies (*see pages 68–69*). Mother of thousands is encouraged by the same things as moss, so good drainage will limit its vigor. Or you could just learn to like it—after all, it's green and flat.

Mother of thousands *Soleirolia soleirolii*
↕ 4 in (10 cm) ✿ late spring–late fall

PEARLWORT

Is there a more unlovely weed? I doubt it. Pearlwort flowers are tiny, with white or often no petals. It's easily mistaken for moss, especially when growing mixed with moss, as it often does.

- **How it succeeds** Ubiquitous on paths, in close-mown grass, and in trampled areas generally, it grows rapidly from numerous, very tiny seeds, which are very persistent in soil. Pearlwort creeps over the soil, rooting as it goes.

- **What to do** Pearlwort's growth habit makes it virtually impossible to hand pull, since some bits of stem and root are always left behind. For the same reason, hoeing is difficult except when plants are small, and it will always come back from seeds in the soil. On the other hand, its small size and tiny seeds make it very susceptible to mulching and competition from other plants. Vigorous grass and not mowing too closely should control it in lawns.

Pearlwort *Sagina procumbens*
↕ 8 in (20 cm) ✿ late spring–mid-fall

OXALIS

These weeds are also known as sorrels, but don't confuse them with true sorrels (the herbs *Rumex acetosa* and *R. scutatus*). There are many weedy oxalis, with yellow or pink flowers, and they include some of the most intractable of all weeds.

- **How they succeed** *O. corniculata* is the commonest species, and one of the most annoying greenhouse weeds. It spreads by stolons and explosive seedpods. The pink-flowered species are bad weeds of cultivated soils, spreading by numerous small bulbils produced at their bases.

- **What to do** You can control *O. corniculata* by persistent hoeing, hand weeding, or flame-weeding, but it tends to come back from seed, so prevention of seeding is a priority. The pink-flowered species are very hard to contain; very determined hoeing might work, but a thick mulch or weed-suppressing membrane is the only certain treatment.

- **Silver lining** All the weedy oxalis species started out as ornamentals and they do have pretty flowers. Don't assume that every pink-flowered oxalis is a weed; *O. articulata* lacks bulbils and is quite well-behaved.

From top: **yellow-flowered oxalis** *Oxalis corniculata*; **pink-flowered oxalis** *O. corymbosa* var. *debilis;* both ↕ 8 in (20 cm) ✿ midsummer–mid-fall

CREEPING BENT

This is one of several perennial grasses that are OK as long as they stay in the lawn, but can cause quite a lot of trouble if they escape. Red fescue (*Festuca rubra*) and common bent (*Agrostis capillaris*), both fine grasses, behave very similarly.

- **How it succeeds** The grass is very widespread in lawns, road shoulders, and waste ground. It grows rapidly, spreads vigorously by stolons, and has tiny, long-persisting seeds. Creeping bent is rarely sown as a lawn grass, but generally ends up being quite abundant in lawns anyway. From there it spreads into surrounding flower beds.

- **What to do** In bare soil, hoeing and hand pulling are both effective, especially when the weeds are young. Once creeping bent and other grasses get mixed up with herbaceous plants, control is much more difficult. Just pulling or cutting the visible leaves and stems is useless; the only solution is get to the root of the matter and remove the entire plant. It is vital to stop grasses in lawns seeding.

- **Silver lining** When closely mown, creeping bent forms a dense, fine turf, greatly valued for putting greens.

Creeping bent *Agrostis stolonifera*
↕ 18 in (45 cm) ✿ midsummer–early fall

FIELD HORSETAIL

This plant, or one very like it, has been around since before the dinosaurs, so it's not surprising that it's so hard to kill. The odd, fir-tree-like shoots are preceded by short-lived, brownish, fertile shoots topped by spore-bearing cones. Horsetail, a distant relative of ferns, has neither leaves nor flowers.

- **How it succeeds** It thrives in fields, hedges, waste places, and gardens—on all soils. New plants grow from the small tubers or any piece of the deep, far-creeping rhizomes. In one experiment, a 4-inch (10-cm) piece of rhizome produced 210 feet (64 m) of new rhizome in a year.

- **What to do** This is difficult to control, since the rhizomes are too deep to dig out. Weed-suppressing membrane is effective, but may take 3–4 years. You can weaken it, but not kill it, by regular hoeing. Horsetail is neither tall nor shade-tolerant, so can be contained, but not eradicated, by a dense planting of tall perennials or shrubs.

- **Did you know?** The shoots are rich in silica, making them feel like sandpaper, and were used for scouring pans. Stems boiled in water are said to be an effective fungicide.

Field horsetail *Equisetum arvense* ↕ 3 ft (1 m)
✿ mid–late-spring. Inset: **fertile shoots** appear first.

GROUND-ELDER

A strong candidate for the most-feared garden weed in many regions, this was described simply by one gardener as "ineradicable." Despite the name and appearance, it is unrelated to the shrubby elder.

- **How it succeeds** It grows abundantly at roadsides and woodland edges, in hedges, waste places, and gardens. The rapidly spreading rhizomes can extend nearly a yard per year. Ground-elder can also spread by seed.

- **What to do** Persistent hoeing will weaken the plant, but not kill it. The rhizomes are brittle and the plant will re-grow from any fragment. They are shallow, so digging them out is theoretically possible, but ground-elder's habit of creeping among other plants makes hoeing and digging difficult. Weed-suppressing membrane is the best option.

- **Did you know?** Ground-elder was introduced to England by the Romans as a pot-herb and for its supposed medicinal properties. It is edible, but hardly recommended. The white flowers are not unattractive and, if you can learn to love it, it is certainly good at suppressing other weeds!

Ground-elder *Aegopodium podagraria*
↕ 3 ft (1 m) ✿ late spring–late summer

EVERGREEN BUGLOSS

Yet another weed that started out as a garden plant, this is now rarely grown. Astonishingly, plants are still commercially available.

- **How it succeeds** Common in hedges and waste places, this weed likes sun, but will tolerate some shade. It is not invasive, but has a deep taproot and readily self-seeds if allowed to flower.

- **What to do** Bugloss is really quite attractive and not all that badly behaved, but is quite hard to get rid of once established. Dig out as much of the root as possible, because it will regrow from any part left behind. Deadhead to prevent it from self-seeding. For gardeners who want a well-behaved alternative to bugloss (and forget-me-nots), try *Brunnera macrophylla*.

- **Warning!** Wear gloves while weeding—like most members of the borage family, the plant is covered in bristly hairs.

Evergreen bugloss *Pentaglottis sempervirens*
↕ 3 ft (1 m) ❋ late spring–midsummer

DOCKS

There are a few common weedy docks, including bitter dock (*Rumex obtusifolius*), but don't worry about telling them apart; from a gardening perspective, they're equally troublesome and ugly.

- **How they succeed** Abundant in cultivated ground, waste places, and road shoulders, they have deep, tough taproots and produce huge amounts of seed. Under good conditions, a single dock plant can produce 30,000 seeds. The seeds can survive in the soil for up to a century. In a recent study in the UK, dock seeds were found in small samples of soil from a third of the gardens tested.

- **What to do** Seedlings can be killed by hoeing, but soon develop taproots and become difficult to kill. Large plants can be killed by digging out the top 6 inches (15 cm) of the taproots, because the plants cannot resprout from the deeper portions. It's vital to stop seed production, so cut down the flowering stems, even if you can't face digging them out.

- **Silver lining** When young, dock leaves are edible, but only just—do not confuse them with the closely related, and much nicer, herb sorrel (*Rumex acetosa*).

From left: **red-veined dock** *Rumex sanguineus*; **curly dock** *Rumex crispus* seedling and flowering plant; both species ↕ 3 ft. (1 m) ✿ early summer–late fall

CREEPING THISTLE

One or two other thistles can turn up in gardens occasionally, but creeping thistle is the only one that is likely to be a serious problem.

- **How it succeeds** Common everywhere, this thistle springs up on pasture, stream banks, and roadsides, at woodland edges, in waste spaces and gardens, and on all soils. The spreading roots may be found at least a few feet below the surface and the plant can regenerate from even small fragments. Creeping thistle can also spread by seed, but this is not normally a problem in gardens.

- **What to do** Hoeing or shallow cultivation will weaken the weed, but will only eradicate it if you are prepared to be very persistent. Digging out is effective, but small pieces of the brittle roots will always be left behind, so be on the lookout for regrowth.

- **Silver lining** The flowers of creeping thistle are popular with bees and butterflies, but that isn't a good reason for letting it flower.

Creeping thistle *Cirsium arvense*
↕ 4 ft (1.2 m) ✿ midsummer–mid-fall

QUACKGRASS

Among grass weeds of cool climates, quackgrass is in a class of its own; no other grass causes half as much trouble.

- **How it succeeds** It is widespread on roadsides and in arable fields, waste spaces, and gardens, on most soils. Fast-growing rhizomes are quackgrass's chief weapon. Excavation of one single plant revealed 505 feet (154 m) of rhizome, giving rise to 206 shoots above ground. Every piece of rhizome with a bud can grow into a new plant.

- **What to do** Persistent hoeing will weaken quackgrass, but eradication requires digging out the rhizomes. Fortunately, this is relatively easy, since they are rarely more than 8 inches (20 cm) deep.

  Dig with a fork, loosening the soil as you go, and you may be able to pull out long, intact lengths of rhizome. Don't use a spade, which will only chop up the rhizomes and make your job more difficult. Quackgrass doesn't produce many seeds and these do not survive for long in the soil.

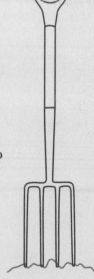

Quackgrass *Elytrigia repens* ↕ 49 in (125 cm) ✿ early summer–mid-fall

RAGWORT

A tall biennial, producing a large, cabbage-like rosette of ragged or divided leaves in its first year, and prodigious quantities of very effectively wind-dispersed seeds in its second. This is not to be confused with Oxford ragwort (*Senecio squalidus*), the ubiquitous urban weed.

- **How it succeeds** Ragwort is a classic colonist of roadsides, waste ground, and neglected grassland. Although it can't flower in mown grass, the rosettes may persist in lawns for years. Ragwort has excellent powers of wind dispersal, easily on a par with dandelion. The foliage, if eaten, is toxic to horses and other livestock.

- **What to do** You can easily prevent it from establishing by dense planting and can kill seedlings by hoeing. Larger plants form deep roots; dig them out before they can seed. Wear gloves when handling live or dead plants.

- **Silver lining** The striped caterpillars of the brightly colored cinnabar moth will often be seen feeding in large numbers on ragwort.

Ragwort *Senecio jacobaea* ‡ 49 in (125 cm) ✿ early summer–late fall

WILLOWHERBS

Several of the smaller willowherbs are problematic garden weeds, of which fringed and broad-leaved willowherb are the commonest. Fireweed is much larger and less common in gardens, but troublesome where it occurs.

- **How they succeed** The smaller willowherbs can turn up anywhere their tiny seeds can germinate. Fireweed is more a plant of woodland edges and waste spaces and a colonist after fires. All willowherbs produce vast numbers of tiny, very effectively wind-dispersed seeds. Fireweed also spreads by creeping roots.

- **What to do** The seeds need bare ground to germinate, so none will successfully invade a densely planted garden. Hoe or hand pull young plants; dig out older plants to make sure no roots remain. Digging out an established fireweed is more difficult, but possible—the roots are not deep.

- **Silver lining** Fireweed is really quite attractive, and a form with white flowers is occasionally grown as a garden plant. It's also the food plant of the elephant hawk moth.

Clockwise from top left: **fireweed** *Chamerion angustifolium* ‡ 5 ft (1.5 m) ✿ midsummer–mid-fall; **broad-leaved willowherb** *Epilobium montanum* ‡ 30 in (75 cm) ✿ early summer–early fall; **fringed willowherb** *Epilobiumciliatum* ‡ 30 in (75 cm) ✿ early summer–early fall

NETTLES

The familiar nettle is a tall perennial with stinging hairs. Less common is its annual relative (*Urtica urens*), usually smaller and more branched. Don't confuse either with deadnettles (*Lamium*).

- **How they succeed** Nettles are famously plants of moist, nutrient-rich soils, often thriving by compost heaps, on riverbanks and old bonfire sites. The perennial tolerates shade and spreads rapidly by underground rhizomes to form large clumps. Both nettles are extremely fast-growing and have long-persistent seeds.

- **What to do** Annual nettle control is the same as for all small-seeded annuals: Prevent germination with a mulch or dense planting and hoe the seedlings, making sure to prevent plants from seeding. Perennial nettle rhizomes are shallow and not very brittle, so are quite easy to dig out with a fork.

- **Silver lining** Nettles have a long history as food, cooked like spinach or made into soup with oats. The fibers were used, like flax, to make string and cloth. Use the nutrient-rich leaves like comfrey as a compost activator or steeped in water to make fertilizer.

Perennial nettle *Urtica dioica* ↕ 5 ft (1.5 m)
✿ early summer—early fall

JAPANESE KNOTWEED

This immigrant is now the tallest herbaceous perennial in the UK. Remarkably, it has colonized the entire country without seeding, since all the plants are genetically parts of a single female, the male being unknown in the country. Much of the initial spread doubtless occurred when the plant was originally promoted as a valuable ornamental.

- **How it succeeds** Japanese knotweed forms large patches on roadsides, waste ground, and riverbanks, and in churchyards. It can spread only from fragments of rhizome, so is not very contagious. On the other hand, once established, its network of tough, fast-growing rhizomes makes it extremely difficult to control.

- **What to do** Ruthlessly cutting down or bashing the stems will help to contain knotweed, but won't kill it. An impervious layer of carpet or similar and plenty of patience seems the best solution.

- **Warning!** Japanese knotweed is rightly regarded as one of the world's most pernicious invasive plants.

Japanese knotweed *Fallopia japonica*
↕ 6 ft (2 m) ✿ late summer–mid-fall

BRAMBLES

Brambles are a complex bunch. Not only are there many species, at least 50 of them grown in gardens, but the native blackberry has a peculiar habit of producing seeds without fertilization, so seedlings are usually exact copies of the parent. Hundreds of "microspecies" result, with very variable fruits: some are delicious, others sour and seedy.

- **How they succeed** Ubiquitous in scrub, woodland edges, waste ground, and hedges, they grow very quickly; their long shoots root where the tips touch the ground. The seeds are widely dispersed by birds and persist in soil.

- **What to do** The only way is to cut down and dig them out. Wear stout gloves and clothing against the thorns. All ornamental brambles can be invasive, so think twice before growing them, especially in a small garden. *Rubus tricolor*, with glossy leaves and very bristly stems, is sold as far-spreading, impenetrable ground cover, which it certainly is.

- **Silver lining** The best bramble microspecies have delicious fruits. Many ornamental species also have edible fruit. Bramble thickets give excellent cover for nesting birds.

Blackberry *Rubus fruticosus* ↕ 6 ft (2 m) ✿ late spring–mid-fall. Inset: **creeping bramble** *Rubus tricolor* ↕ 20 in (50 cm) ✿ early–late summer

BINDWEEDS

Hedge, large, and field bindweed are all extremely intractable climbing weeds. Hedge (*Calystegia sepium*) and large bindweed are very similar and often hybridize; in fact, in some areas the hybrid is commoner than either. Field bindweed is a smaller plant, but no less troublesome.

- **How they succeed** All are common in hedges, waste ground, gardens, and woodland edges. Field bindweed also invades arable crops. The bindweeds spread by fleshy, brittle rhizomes. Seeds persist for a long time in soil, but fortunately are rarely produced.

- **What to do** Persistent cultivation will weaken them, but is unlikely to kill them. Digging out is not effective: The rhizomes are deep and easily break into fragments, each of which can produce a new plant. An impervious weed-suppressing membrane is the only practical solution.

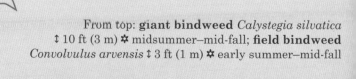

- **Silver lining** All bindweeds have attractive flowers, but it is best to admire them in someone else's garden.

From top: **giant bindweed** *Calystegia silvatica* ↕ 10 ft (3 m) ✿ midsummer–mid-fall; **field bindweed** *Convolvulus arvensis* ↕ 3 ft (1 m) ✿ early summer–mid-fall

GIANT HOGWEED

This is another weed that, like Japanese knotweed, started out as a garden plant. However, giant hogweed is rarely a problem in gardens, although it's very troublesome in the wider countryside. It is possibly the tallest herbaceous plant in Europe.

- **How it succeeds** This weed forms large colonies on riverbanks and occasionally on waste ground. On moist, fertile soils, giant hogweed's large seeds, rapid growth, and extremely large size can quickly overwhelm all other vegetation. A single large plant may produce 20,000 seeds.

- **What to do** You're unlikely to acquire giant hogweed accidentally, so the simple solution is not to grow it. It's a biennial, so cutting it down before it sets seed will stop it from spreading, but severing the root below ground is the only sure way to prevent regrowth. The seeds do not persist in the soil. Giant hogweed is prohibited in some states. For something equally striking but less troublesome, try giant fennel (*Ferula communis*).

- **Warning!** Giant hogweed sap causes skin blistering on exposure to sunlight.

Giant hogweed *Heracleum mantegazzianum*
↕ 11 ft (3.5 m) ✿ early–late summer

Garden thugs

Most weeds are uninvited guests; the plants described here are (or were) deliberately brought into gardens as ornamentals, but have thuggish habits.

BULBS AND CORMS

Many beautiful garden plants have corms (swollen underground stems) or bulbs (made from fleshy leaves), but some can prove troublesome. Here are two of my favorite villains.

Three-cornered leek is one of many alliums grown in gardens. It originates from southwest Europe and is now a weed in mild climates from California to New Zealand. It's very attractive, but I think you would have to be crazy to grow it in the first place.

It spreads both by seed and by numerous small bulbs, which are easily transported in soil. Digging it out is possible, but it's easy to miss the smallest of the bulbs. A very minor consolation is that the entire plant is edible; it has a mild onion or garlic flavor.

Coppertip is a sterile, cormous hybrid of two South African species and, along with Japanese knotweed (*see page 140*), is proof that lacking seeds is no barrier to rapid spread. If you want an orange-flowered perennial that takes care of itself, then by all means go ahead and grow it, but there are many cultivars that are more attractive and much better behaved. Try 'Citronella,' 'Solfatare,' and (with the largest flowers of all) 'Emily McKenzie.'

Left to right: **three-cornered leek** *Allium triquetrum* ↕ 18 in (45 cm) ✿ mid-spring–early summer; **coppertip** *Crocosmia x crocosmiiflora* ↕ 24 in (60 cm) ✿ midsummer–early fall

HERBACEOUS PERENNIALS

Approach these (and many other) perennials with considerable caution: They spread with remarkable speed, either by seed or vegetative means.

Yellow loosestrife builds up an impenetrable network of rhizomes below ground and a dense stand of leafy stems above ground. Control by digging out the rhizomes (but any piece left behind will produce a new plant). You could keep it in poor soil, to reduce its vigor, but the best solution is not to grow it in the first place. There are better (and better-behaved) forms, such as *Lysimachia ciliata* 'Firecracker.'

Welsh poppy produces huge numbers of tiny seeds that persist in the soil. Seedlings quickly produce deep taproots and are difficult to uproot—kill them by hoeing. Ruthless deadheading will prevent seeding and mulch or dense planting should prevent seeds from germinating.

Goldenrod spreads by rhizomes and, if you let it, by abundant, wind-dispersed seeds, but it is an excellent nectar plant for bees and butterflies; *Solidago gigantea* is similar. Control them as for yellow loosestrife or choose modern cultivars, which are shorter and much less invasive.

Clockwise from left: **yellow loosestrife** *Lysimachia punctata* ‡ 4 ft (1.2 m) ✿ mid-summer–late fall; **Welsh poppy** *Meconopsis cambrica* ‡ 24 in (60 cm) ✿ summer–early fall; **goldenrod** *Solidago canadensis* ‡ 6 ft (2 m) ✿ late summer–fall

COMFREY

This is the plant for which the word "coarse" might have been especially coined: Comfrey is tall, leafy, and covered with bristly hairs (these are irritating to some people with sensitive skin).

- **How it succeeds** It grows in any moist, fertile soil, likes sun but will tolerate some shade, and forms large, spreading clumps. Some comfrey species, such as *Symphytum officinalis*, and hybrids are more invasive than others, but all are deep-rooted and tough to get rid of once established. They will regrow from fragments of root and self-seed if you let them flower.

- **What to do** Cut down comfrey regularly to help control it and stop it from flowering. *Symphytum* x *uplandicum* 'Bocking 14' is sterile and doesn't produce seeds.

- **Silver lining** If you believe some organic gardeners, comfrey is the botanical equivalent to the philosopher's stone. Bees love the blue, pink, or white flowers. The leaves are used as compost activator and to make liquid fertilizer and remedies for various disorders, especially sprains and broken bones ("knitbone" is comfrey's old country name).

Comfrey *Symphytum caucasicum* ↕ 4¹/₂ ft (1.35 m) ✿ early summer–early fall. Inset: **white-flowered form** invading lawn.

GRASSES

Grasses, a group that includes the bamboos, are increasingly popular garden plants. Many of them are well-behaved—but some are not.

Reed canary grass, a variegated grass, is one of those old-fashioned, "pass-along" garden plants that everyone acquires when their neighbors are throwing some out. It spreads vigorously by means of rhizomes and is best physically contained if you don't want to spend time controlling it.

Bamboo Some bamboos form neat clumps, while others spread aggressively. *Sasa veitchii*, like all members of the *Sasa* genus, is the invasive kind. It thrives in most soils and full sun to moderate shade and spreads by underground rhizomes. You can snap off new shoots that appear where you don't want them while they are still small. Otherwise dig down, sever the rhizome, and remove the unwanted parts.

A more effective method is to install a physical barrier on planting, for example corrugated iron or paving slabs. The rhizomes will go straight through any less substantial barrier, such as a butyl pond liner. Even better still, grow a more well-behaved bamboo like *Fargesia* or *Phyllostachys*.

Reed canary grass *Phalaris arundinacea* var. *picta* ↕ 3 ft (1 m) ✿ summer. Inset: **bamboo** *Sasa veitchii* ↕ 4–6 ft (1.2–2 m).

SHRUBS

Most garden shrubs are quite well-behaved, at least in the sense that they stay where you put them, but here are four that don't. The solution, unless you actually enjoy trying to tame plants with no sense of proportion, is not to grow them in the first place.

Large periwinkle Undoubtedly very attractive, this short, spreading shrub thrives in most soils and tolerates shade. The flowers unfurl like an umbrella. Its fast-growing, looping stems root where they touch the ground. Although it is not a tall plant on its own, its scrambling habit enables it to grow over and swamp taller plants.

Periwinkle's growth habit makes it hard to restrain, but it's not difficult to dig out if you're sufficiently determined. Lesser periwinkle (*Vinca minor*), especially some of its more choice cultivars such as the white-flowered 'Gertrude Jekyll,' is less invasive. If you really must have large periwinkle, grow the less vigorous, variegated form.

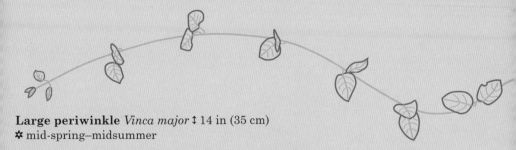

Large periwinkle *Vinca major* ↕ 14 in (35 cm)
✿ mid-spring–midsummer

Rose of Sharon may well be sold to you as useful ground cover for a dry, shady bank where nothing else will grow, but turn your back on it for a moment and the chances are that it will run amok.

Salal Given a moderately damp climate, an acidic soil, and some shade, there are no limits to the territorial ambitions of salal (otherwise known as shallon). It has sometimes been grown as cover for game on large estates— the best place for it. Salal has no place in a small garden.

From left: **rose of Sharon** *Hypericum calycinum* ↕ 24 in (60 cm) ✿ early-summer– early fall; **salal** *Gaultheria shallon* ↕ 5 ft (1.5 m) ✿ late spring–midsummer

Snowberry is a suckering shrub that owes its widespread distribution in the UK to having been planted as cover for game. It is tatty, invasive, scarcely attractive, and best avoided. The edible fruits are hardly worth the effort, but children (of all ages) enjoy throwing them at each other.

Sumac In many respects, sumac is an ideal tree for a small garden, with elegant foliage and brilliant fall color. But its startling ability to throw up vigorous suckers from its roots means that you will be forever digging them up.

From left: **snowberry** *Symphoricarpos albus* ↕ 6 ft (2 m) ✿ early summer–mid-fall; **sumac** *Rhus typhina* ↕ 16 ft (5 m) ✿ early summer–early winter

Warm-climate weeds

Like annual weeds in hot, dry regions (*see pages 108–11*), Johnsongrass and nutsedge photosynthesize more efficiently to grow faster.

Yellow nutsedge has a rather grassy appearance, but its true nature is betrayed by its triangular, sedge stem (grass stems are flat or round). Nutsedge's secret weapons are its spreading rhizomes and small tubers, which make it very difficult to control.

Hoeing and digging out helps, but for real control, use a weed-suppressing membrane or very thick organic mulch. If you stop them from growing, most tubers in the soil decay within two years and none survive beyond four or five seasons. Nutsedge is quite short and a poor competitor, so dense planting of perennials or shrubs helps to subdue it.

When I was young, nutsedge tubers were widely sold as a chewy snack (called "tiger nuts"), but now seem to be available only as a health food (high in protein, minerals, and vitamins) or—oddly—as fishing bait. Apparently carp can't resist them!

Johnsongrass, a very tall, fast-growing, rhizomatous grass, is officially one of the world's 10 worst weeds. It hails from Mediterranean Europe, but its name commemorates

Left to right: **Johnsongrass** *Sorghum halepense* ↕ 6 ft (2 m) ✿ midsummer–mid-fall; **yellow nutsedge** *Cyperus esculentus* ↕ 20 in (50 cm) ✿ midsummer–early fall

the luckless farmer who introduced it to Alabama from South Carolina in the 1840s. A single plant can cover 20 square yards (17 sq. m) in two years and produce 28,000 seeds. Control requires diligent removal of the plants, while trying as hard as possible to dig up all traces of rhizome. (Hand pulling mature plants is difficult; the leaves have sharp edges, so wear gloves.) Once it's mostly under control, use a weed-suppressing membrane to keep it that way.

Lawn weeds

Lawns and weeds go together like bread and butter. Here are some of the best.

DAISY

This is a true lawn specialist, more or less confined to this habitat in gardens. The flowers open during the day, hence the name, a contraction of "day's eye."

- **How it succeeds** With its flat rosette of leaves and short, leafless flowering stems, daisies can easily duck under even the closest mowing. Abundant, tiny seeds are produced throughout the summer.

- **What to do** Daisies cannot tolerate competition from taller plants, so keeping a dense, vigorous sward and not mowing too closely will keep them from getting out of hand. Remove individual plants with a knife or daisy grubber.

- **Silver lining** Who could really dislike a plant with such a delightful name in both English and French (*paquerette* or little Easter flower)? No one should grow up without making a daisy chain.

Daisy *Bellis perennis* ↕ 3 in (8 cm) ❀ early spring–late fall

FIELD WOODRUSH

Here is living proof that there is no such thing as a free lunch. Most other common lawn weeds prefer neutral or alkaline soil, so can be discouraged by making your lawn more acidic. Unfortunately, field woodrush positively thrives on acidic soil.

- **How it succeeds** Field woodrush closely resembles lawn grasses (apart from the long hairs on the edges of its leaves) and, like them, its leaves grow from the base, enabling it to continue growing after mowing. It flowers and sets seeds in spring, often before mowing begins, and also spreads by short stolons.

- **What to do** Small infestations can be dug out, but the only long-term answer is to add lime to the soil to raise its pH and make it less acidic. On the other hand, field woodrush doesn't look a lot different from grass, so why not just tolerate it?

Field woodrush *Luzula campestris* ‡ 6 in (15 cm)
✤ early spring–midsummer

COMMON PLANTAIN

Another lawn specialist, common plantain has a flat rosette of leaves and short, leafless flowering stems. Hoary plantain (*Plantago media*) is sometimes found in lawns on limestone, but is a far more attractive plant. Narrowleaf plantain is also very common, but is rather taller and less at home in closely mowed grass.

- **How it succeeds** A very fast-growing plant, common plantain is also extremely tolerant of trampling and soil compaction, so is very common on paths. Abundant seeds are produced, even when it is regularly mowed, and are long-lived in the soil.

- **What to do** Dig up individual plants; as long as the crown is removed, the plant will not regrow from any roots left in the soil. Like all really prostrate lawn weeds, vigorous and not-too-short grass helps to control it.

- **Did you know?** So reliably did this plantain follow European colonization that native Americans, and the poet Longfellow in *Hiawatha*, called it "white man's foot."

Narrowleaf plantain *Plantago lanceolata* ↕ 12 in (30 cm) ✿ mid-spring–early fall. Inset: **common plantain** *P. major* ↕ 6 in (15 cm) ✿ late spring–mid-fall.

LESSER TREFOIL, WHITE CLOVER

The stems of these related and perfectly adapted lawn weeds creep along below the mower blades.

- **How they succeed** White clover spreads by stolons, or runners, that root as they grow. In a fertile soil with no competition, one single shoot produced 157 feet (48 m) of stolons in a year, although they don't achieve anything like that in the average lawn. Lesser trefoil also creeps, but is an annual and grows from a single root. Both produce abundant, long-lived seeds.

- **What to do** There's really no satisfactory organic treatment for white clover, although raking before mowing can help to remove some stems. It is not easily dispersed, and lawns established without it may never acquire it.

  Because each plant of lesser trefoil, however large, is rooted in one place, if there are few plants, it's possible to cut the root and pull out each whole plant.

  Both plants fix their own nitrogen and do best if the grass is thin and poor. They are less vigorous, and less obvious, if the sward is kept dense and well fed.

- **Silver lining** White clover is a favorite with bees.

From top: **lesser trefoil** *Trifolium dubium* ↕ 6 in (15 cm) ✿ late spring–late fall; **white clover** *T. repens* ↕ 8 in (20 cm) ✿ early summer–mid-fall

DANDELION

Too familiar to need describing, dandelions (like brambles) produce seeds without fertilization, leading to the evolution of hundreds of very slightly differing plants or "microspecies." Two other dandelion-like plants turn up quite often in lawns: cat's ear, on acidic soils, and also various hawkbits (*Leontodon* species).

- **How it succeeds** Dandelions are fast-growing and adaptable, being able to remain quite flat in lawns but more erect in taller vegetation. The rosettes are very tolerant of trampling. Huge numbers of the small, wind-dispersed seeds are produced in early summer.

- **What to do** Seedlings are easily killed by hoeing or hand weeding when young, but neither method is really an option in lawns. You can dig out the taproot, but take care to remove all of it—any piece can grow into a new plant.

- **Silver lining** Dandelions have almost too many uses to list. They increasingly turn up in salads with mixtures of other leaves and can be stir-fried, pickled, or cooked with pasta or in pies. Rabbits adore them. Wine can be made from the flowers, the roasted roots have been used as a coffee substitute, and latex from the roots has been made into rubber. Dandelion is a well-known diuretic, hence the French name of *pissenlit* (piss-the-bed).

Left to right: **cat's ear** *Hypochaeris radicata* ‡ 24 in (60 cm) ✿ early summer–mid-fall; **dandelion** *Taraxacum officinale* ‡ 12 in (30 cm) ✿ early spring–late fall

YARROW

Yarrow spreads slowly to form dark-green, drought-resistant patches of finely divided, feathery leaves in lawns. Flowering stems are too tall to survive in lawns unless mowing is neglected for a long time.

- **How it succeeds** Yarrow is very common in grassland, and by roadsides and hedges. It spreads by shallow underground rhizomes.

- **What to do** Like many lawn weeds, yarrow competes best with thin, starved grass. A dense, vigorous sward should prevent it from spreading, even if it doesn't actually kill it. Raking before mowing helps, and the shallow rhizomes can be pulled out if you're careful.

- **Silver lining** If yarrow is a serious problem, consider giving up completely and establishing a yarrow lawn as an alternative to a chamomile lawn. Yarrow foliage is aromatic when crushed (fragrant or offensive, depending on who you believe) and the flowers are pretty, so your lawn will still look attractive if you stop mowing for a while. Of course, then you'll have to control the grass....

Yarrow *Achillea millefolium* ↕ 18 in (45 cm) ✿ early summer–early fall

CREEPING BUTTERCUP

There are three very common (and very similar), yellow-flowered buttercups, but creeping buttercup is the only one with creeping stems and the only one likely to cause trouble in gardens.

- **How it succeeds** Buttercups are common in cultivated soil, lawns, grassland, and waste places—on all soils. Fast-growing runners enable a single plant to cover 43 square feet (4 sq. m) in a year, although plants in lawns won't achieve this. The seeds can survive in soil for many decades.

- **What to do** Seedlings can be killed by hoeing. Newly rooted runners can be pulled up, but established plants need to be dug out. Raking before mowing will lift up runners so they can be cut off by the blades. As usual, vigorous, not-too-short grass will help keep them in check.

Creeping buttercup *Ranunculus repens*
↕ 24 in (60 cm) ✿ late spring–early fall

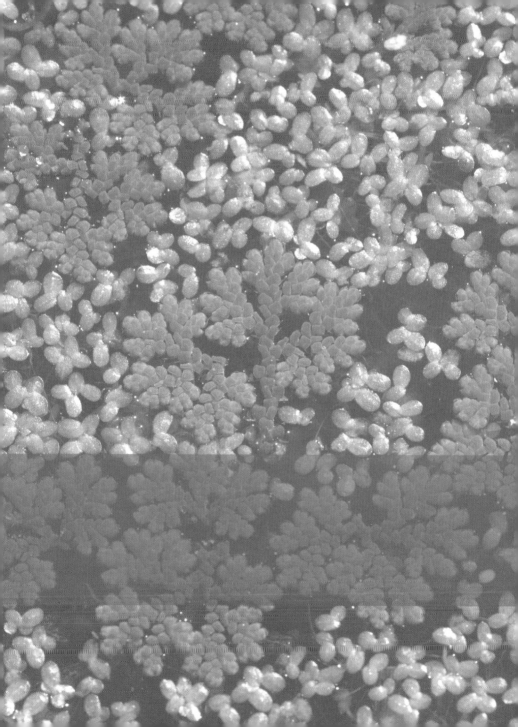

Rogues' gallery: water weeds Floating, choking, or spreading

BLANKET WEED & MOSQUITOFERN

Most weeds are flowering plants, but here are two more primitive plants: an aquatic fern and an alga.

Blanket weed The commonest is *Cladophora*, but there are several other genera. Blanket weeds are filamentous algae (algae consisting of strands of cells), but single-celled algae can also turn your pond water green. You can remove them with a rake or by wrapping them around a stick, or you can use proprietary chemical treatments. However, not only is prevention much better than cure, it's also very easy.

All algae are encouraged by lots of sunshine and nutrient-rich water, so the key is to reduce both. Ensure that at least half your pond's surface is covered by floating aquatics or water lilies (ironically, duckweed is good at this). Avoid using fertilizers in ponds or anywhere they can run off into the water, prevent leaves and debris from falling into the water, and if you have fish, feed them sparingly.

Mosquitofern is a small, floating fern that starts out green, but may turn red in summer. It's controlled in much the same way as duckweed (*see page 180*), but the best solution is not to acquire it in the first place. It should no longer be found on sale, so make sure that you don't get it, by accident or design, when accepting water plants from friends.

From top: **blanket weed** *Cladophora;*
Pacific mosquitofern *Azolla filiculoides*

DUCKWEED

This is an extremely common floating water weed. Flowering is very rare, and you probably wouldn't notice anyway. A dense covering can make a pond look solid; it's possible to be fooled and end up getting wet or even drowning.

- **How it succeeds** Given plenty of sun and nutrient-rich water, duckweed grows at an alarming rate. It is easily moved around with water plants and by frogs or birds. A single piece is enough to start an infestation.

- **What to do** Avoid getting duckweed in the first place—inspect new water plants carefully to check for its presence. If your pond has it, rake it out (a toy rake is ideal), leave it on smooth paving or plastic by the pond edge to allow any animal inhabitants to return to the water, and add it to the compost heap. Don't leave it on pebbles or gravel, since it's hard to get off again. Or you could always get a duck....

- **Silver lining** Duckweed does shade the water beneath, which helps to control blanket weed.

Duckweed *Lemna minor*

INVASIVE FLOATING WATER WEEDS

New Zealand pigmyweed, floating pennywort, and parrot feather are extremely fast-growing water plants that will soon spread over a pond to form choking mats. The best solution is not to grow them in the first place, but there are several things that you can do to stop them from taking over.

From left: **New Zealand pigmyweed** *Crassula helmsii* ‡ 4 in (10 cm);
floating pennywort *Hydrocotyle ranunculoides* ‡ 8 in (20 cm);
parrot feather *Myriophyllum aquaticum* ‡ 8 in (20 cm)

What to do:

- If you have any of them already, rake them out and put them on the compost heap—never put them in the trash or dump them in the wild.
- If your pond has a stream outlet, it's absolutely essential to prevent any pieces from being washed downstream.
- If you find any of them still on sale, ask the retailer why.
- Use well-behaved alternatives: These may include white water-crowfoot (*Ranunculus aquatilis*), creeping spearwort (*R. flammula*), coon's tail (*Ceratophyllum demersum*), shortspike watermilfoil (*Myriophyllum spicatum*), and true forget-me-not (*Myosotis scorpioides*).

THUGGISH WATER PLANTS

Many native water plants look very much at home in large ponds and lakes, but it is usually a mistake to grow them in a garden pond. Here are some to avoid.

White water lily A beautiful but also very large water lily; a single plant can completely overwhelm a small pond. Try *Nymphaea tetragona* instead.

Purple loosestrife is a perfectly well-behaved marginal plant in its European homeland. In North America, however, it is overwhelming natural wetlands and is banned in several states.

Yellow flag Another lovely plant, this spreads aggressively to form a network of thick rhizomes. There is a range of less vigorous irises available.

Typha This aggressive, rhizomatous spreader is sometimes called bulrush, but the true bulrush (*Scirpus* species) is unrelated. In the UK, typha is also known as reedmace—which is as misleading as bulrush, since this plant is neither a reed nor a rush. *Typha minima* is a less thuggish substitute.

Clockwise from top left: **white water lily** *Nymphaea alba* ✿ early summer–early fall; **purple loosestrife** *Lythrum salicaria* ↕ 4 ft (1.2 m) ✿ early summer–early fall; **yellow flag** *Iris pseudacorus* ↕ 5 ft (1.5 m) ✿ late spring–late summer; **typha** *Typha latifolia* ↕ 9 ft (2.75 m) ✿ early–late summer

USEFUL ADDRESSES AND BOOKS

All About Lawns features lots of information about lawn mowing and maintenance, as well as numerous helpful articles about keeping your lawn healthy, beautiful, and weed-free. **www. allaboutlawns.com**

The American Horticultural Society is one of the oldest gardening organizations around. Visit its website for seasonal gardening tips and membership information: **www.ahs.org**

The Biology of Canadian Weeds, Agricultural Institute of Canada (**http://pubs.nrc-cnrc. gc.ca/aic-journals/weeds. html**). This series contains incredibly detailed information about all Canada's main weeds.

The Department of Agriculture has a searchable online database that includes information on where each species grows in the United States, and whether there are any warnings or restrictions on growing them in your area. **http://plants.usda.gov**

Ergonica says it is "probably the largest selection of weed pullers and weed killing hand tools on the Web" (**www. ergonica.com/Garden_Tools. htm**), and I wouldn't disagree.

Missouri Botanical Garden provides advice on an enormous range of gardening problems, including a limited range of weeds. Visit **www. mobot.org/gardeninghelp/ plantinfo.shtml**

The National Gardening Association offers articles and advice, an illustrated weed library, and a useful plant finder that can identify a species based on physical description. See **www.garden.org**

The Pest & Weed Expert

by Dr D.G. Hessayon (Expert, 2007) includes brief advice on how to identify and control the most common garden weeds. **www.amazon.com**

Valley Oak Tool Company

supplies wheel hoes and parts. There is a video on the website that shows how to use them, too: See **www.valleyoaktool.com/ wheelhoe.html**

The Weed Science Society of America works to promote

scientific research, education, and awareness about weeds. **www.wssa.net**

REFERENCES

Christopher Lloyd, *The Well-Tempered Garden*, Weidenfield & Nicolson, 2003, page 26

Richard Mabey, *Food for Free*, Fontana, 1975, pages 83 and 96

RHS Plant Finder, Dorling Kindersley, published annually

Matthew Wilson, *RHS New Gardening*, Mitchell Beazley, 2007, page 42

Small herbs have grace: great weeds do grow apace.

Richard III, II, iv, 13

Index

Acknowledgments

Author's acknowledgments
Thanks to everyone at DK, including Clare Shedden, as well as Alison Donovan, Helen Fewster, and Francesca Gormley. Thanks also to Anna Kruger for having the courage to ask me to write a second book, but as usual a very special thanks to Annelise Evans for all her help and for her lovely, weedy garden.

Thanks to Pat for her love and tolerance of the author at work, and for her sensible refusal to acknowledge that I know any more about weeds than she does.

Publisher's acknowledgments
DK would like to thank the following for allowing us to photograph in their gardens: Cynthia and Trevor Butt, Jane and Michael Cranfield, Sharon and Ivan Gould, Lara Madge, Anne and Richard Ohlenschlager, Lucy and Stuart Riley, Amanda Roberts-Davies, Julia Simmonds, Gill and Chris Watson. Thanks also to Rona Bateman for help in preparing photoshoots.

Photographic credits
DK would like to thank the following for their kind permission to reproduce their photographs:
Key: b-below/bottom; l-left; r-right; t-top
Alamy Images: Arco Images GmbH p.179b; Richard Becker p.36; blickwinkel p.111br; Nigel Cattlin p.161l, pp.176-77; Cubo Images srl p.109r; tbkmedia.de: p.129br; The Garden Picture Library p.182; Pat Tuson p.109l; UK21 p.183l. DK Images: © Barrie Watts p.1. Field Robot Event: p.82. FLPA: Nigel Cattlin p.111tr, 161r. Photolibrary: p.111tl. Niels Proctor: p.119b. Science Photo Library: David Hughes p.111bl. Ken Thompson: p.143 inset. Valley Oak Tool Company: p.56tl.

Jacket images: front and back: iStockphoto.com; Mike Bentley (background); Alina Pavlova (grass).

Most new photography by Peter Anderson; the remainder by Andy Crawford.

All other images © DK Images
For further information, see:
www.dkimages.com